Don McNay's

GREATEST HITS

Ten Years as an Award-Winning Columnist

By Don McNay, CLU, ChFC, MSFS, CSSC

RRP International Publishing LLC
Richmond, Ky. · Greater New Orleans

RRP International LLC, DBA Eugenia Ruth LLC
PO Box 1778,
Richmond, Ky. 40476

www.rrpinternational.org

ISBN-13: 978-0-9898848-3-9

Previous Books by Don McNay:

Son of a Son of a Gambler: Joe McNay 80th Birthday Edition

Life Lessons from the Golf Course: The Quest for Spiritual Meaning, Psychological Understanding and Inner Peace through the Game of Golf (coauthored with Clay Hamrick)

Life Lessons from the Lottery: Protecting Your Money in a Scary World

Wealth Without Wall Street: A Main Street Guide to Making Money

Son of a Son of a Gambler: Winners, Losers and What to Do When You Win the Lottery

The Unbridled World of Ernie Fletcher: Reflections on Kentucky's Governor

www.rrpinternational.org

Dedication

This book is dedicated to Al Smith, Byron Crawford, Joe Nocera, Jim Todd and Arianna Huffington. My journey from being a small town writer to syndicated columnist would not have happened without them.

Table of Contents

Introduction

"There's just too much to see
Waiting in front of me
And I know that I just can't go wrong"
-Jimmy Buffett

It's been one heck of a run.

When I came out of graduate school at Vanderbilt in 1982, I spent three years writing a monthly column for the *Lexington Herald*. One day editor John Carroll said they were dropping all the community columnists.

John went on to win a boatload of Pulitzer Prizes, so it is hard to argue about his editorial judgment. On the other hand, I missed having that forum.

For the next 20 years, I silently wrote columns in my head. I had moved to Richmond, Kentucky, and in November 2003 I mentioned to Jodi Whitaker, the news editor at the local paper, that I had written for the *Herald*. She asked if I would write a piece for their business section.

I wrote about why I hate Yoko Ono. Not a piece on financial planning like they might have been expecting.

Yoko was a hit and I got a weekly, unpaid gig as a columnist for the *Richmond Register*.

At that moment, I felt exactly like the protagonist in the Bruce Springsteen song "Thunder Road." "We got one chance to make it real, trade in these wings on some wheels."

This was my one chance to make it as a writer. I had to give it everything I had.

Kentucky Hall of Fame journalist Byron Crawford, who is one the people I dedicated this book to, did a wonderful Fourth of July 2006 piece about me in the *Louisville Courier-Journal* and said that "I had a need to speak my mind."

I did.

Byron's piece ran in Gannett papers all over the country and played a big role in my being syndicated a few months later.

How I stayed a columnist for 10 years was a combination of divine providence and breaks that would put Forrest Gump to shame.

By accident, I happened to open two of my columns with a rock and roll lyric. I skipped the next week and received a tidal wave of people wondering where it was.

It's been there ever since.

Al Smith hosted an influential television show called *Comment on Kentucky* on Kentucky public television. He had booked me on the show during my first run as a columnist in 1984 and immediately booked me again in 2004.

Al took a lot of flak from establishment journalists for booking a part-time columnist from one of the state's smallest daily papers, but Al, being strong-minded, kept inviting me back and I built up an audience.

When I made my final appearance on *Comment on Kentucky* on September 13, 2013. I said that "I truly love *Comment on Kentucky*, and I truly love Al Smith."

I do.

When I started at the *Register*, the editing and publishing positions were revolving doors, and it was only a matter of time before a new editor dropped me in favor of someone less controversial.

Then Jim Todd was named Richmond's editor.

Jim was a lifetime journalist who had come out of retirement to edit the *Register*. Although he fired me (and rehired me) four or five times and kept the famed first amendment attorney Jon Fleischaker on his speed dial, he never killed or "spiked" one of my columns, even if he did not personally agree with it. He was instrumental in my column getting syndicated.

Jim took a paper that was considered one of Kentucky's worst daily newspapers and won a Kentucky Press Association award for excellence two years later.

I've ended the column at the end of the 10-year run, but it came close to dying in 2007. My mother and sister died and my marriage ended during a nine-month run in 2006. At first, writing was my salvation, but making the weekly deadlines started to be a burden. I sent in a letter of resignation, but Joe Nocera, who is now one of the top opinion columnists in the world at the *New York Times*, convinced me to hang on and take it back.

I was still undecided, but in July 2008, I had gone to Washington DC to see a client for my structured settlement business. I found that Joe would be in town the next day. I stayed around an extra day to have breakfast with him and on a day when the temperature hit 104 degrees, I dropped into the Newseum, primarily because it had air conditioning.

I happened to see Arianna Huffington in the Newseum and that chance meeting led to my writing for the *Huffington Post* two months later. With *Huffington*, I suddenly had a large international audience just as the world economy was collapsing and when trained economic writers were in big demand.

I had the unusual niche of being a traditional Democrat totally opposed to the Wall Street bailouts. Huffington gave me a forum that decision makers had to take seriously.

The exposure was also a boost for my career. All my books are now bestsellers, even those unrelated to economics or politics. My expertise in what to do when you win the lottery captured worldwide attention.

So why am I leaving?

Although the logical answer is that after 10 years this was a chance to go out on top, it is actually a little more complicated. I'm going into the book publishing business in a big manner, the way you see actors go into producing and directing.

Clint Eastwood is an example. The things he has done as a director far outshine his acting career, but he is able to go back and forth from one to the other. I plan on making that same kind of back and forth between publishing and continuing to write books myself.

I have a clear vision where RRP International Publishing, my book publishing business, is headed. The goal is not just to create books, but create stars. I want my authors to be recognized as experts and the goal is to help them draw a large audience.

RRP is a cross between journalism, social media and the way books are currently published and distributed. My goal is to be the *Huffington Post* of book publishing or as my wife calls it, "books without Wall Street." Or at least without the traditional, New York-based publishing model. We are operating out of Kentucky and Greater New Orleans and looking at the world in an entirely different way.

I've always looked outside my universe for role models. Warren Buffett, Steve Jobs and Ted Turner had far more influence on how I set up my settlement planning business than anyone inside that the financial services world. The key to success is business is avoiding the "me too" syndrome of copying your direct competitors.

I listed Chicago columnist Mike Royko as a major influence during my growing years, but my inspiration for writing comes from song writers. Two of my favorites, Jimmy Webb and Janis Ian have become email friends after I used their songs in columns.

The book chapters are separated into categories based on song lyrics and list the years when they appeared in print. That gives you a pretty good idea where my life was at that time.

When I write, I see myself as Jackson Browne, Bruce Springsteen or Adele baring my soul to the world. Since I look like an attorney or an accountant, and many of my friends are actually attorneys and accountants, I surprised a lot of people with the edgy boldness of my deepest thoughts.

Writing a column has been a great privilege. I did it passion and enthusiasm for 10 years.

The results are in the enclosed pages.

Don McNay, CLU, ChFC, MSFS, CSSC
September 2013

Section One

LETS MAKE SOME MONEY

Life Lessons about Money and Happiness
(2013)

When the body of murdered Florida Lotto winner Abraham Shakespeare was found, his mother said that on many occasions Shakespeare said he wished he had torn up the winning ticket.

After lottery winner Jack Whittaker of Hurricane, West Virginia, went through a litany of problems, including the drug overdose death of his granddaughter, his wife, now his ex-wife, wished he had torn up his record-breaking Powerball ticket.

Seems like a lot of lottery winners want to tear up the ticket.

Some don't verbalize the thought. They just run through the money as fast as they can.

Having unlimited wealth is a dream for many people, many who consciously or subconsciously hate the idea of being rich.

What is going on?

A lot of misery comes from not having financial systems in place. The winners weren't ready for their 15 minutes of fame and the hangers-on who would want a piece of them.

People don't really know what to do with wealth. Some dream of showing off or sticking it to people they don't like. While "take this job and shove it" probably feels good for a day, revenge won't keep you happy over the long run.

Money equals security for most people. Or at least it should. One of the primary reasons that people become entrepreneurs is to keep big corporations from running their lives. They want to be responsible for their own financial destiny.

Since money is the ultimate security blanket, it seems senseless that people fritter it away. Yet, it has been said that 90 percent of people who get a lump sum do exactly that.

Some people get tired of pursuing money for money's sake. I've long been fascinated by the story of Millard Fuller, the founder of Habitat for Humanity. Fuller was a millionaire at a very young age. His primary focus was getting rich. His wife was at the point of leaving him. He stepped back and took a look at himself and didn't like what he saw. He and his wife sold everything and moved to a commune-like farm. From there, he redirected his passion and business skills and built an organization that made a profound and lasting impact on society.

I've studied "Big Money" for all of my adult life, and most of the problems come down to a few areas.

First is a person, like Abraham Shakespeare, who just couldn't say no. He was the perfect mark for every con artist with a story.

Usually the person with a story isn't a stranger. It's family, longtime friends and newfound "romantic interests." A lot of emotions get brought into play.

And money seems to flow out the door.

The second is having too much money all at once. Most of the lotto winners who get in trouble are the people who took all the cash up front. If it were up to me, I wouldn't let lottery winners take a "cash option." If they took the annual payments, they would learn from the mistakes with their first installment or two, and would still have 18 or 19 more chances to get it right.

Most lottery winners eventually figure things out, once the money is gone. Or when they are at the point where they wish they had "torn up the ticket."

The government figured it out a long time ago. We don't give people a lump sum social security check at retirement. We don't want them to run out of the money. The same used to hold true with pension plans. People received an annuity that lasted the rest of their lives.

Today, most pensions are 401(k) plans. Just like the lotto winners, people are running out of retirement money while they are still alive.

When you think about it, almost all of us have our own "lotto moment." We make decisions about money that will either give us long-term security and happiness or bring on pain and regret.

Handling a lump sum wisely can be a "ticket to paradise." Or, like Abraham Shakespeare and Powerball Jack, it can be a ticket to misery that they wish they would have torn up.

When to Take a Severance Package
(2010)

"In the end there is once dance you'll do alone"
-Jackson Browne

In 1991, the IBM plant in Lexington, Ky. became Lexmark. IBM offered employee severance packages. People could take the package or take a chance that Lexmark would keep them on.

Several IBM employees came to me for advice. Some took the package and others did not. After seeing that, I concluded that taking a package is an individual decision. There are no set guidelines.

Many of the IBM employees were engineers or had heavy statistical backgrounds. They wanted an answer they could quantify. They sought me to calculate the present value of their package.

After 30 seconds crunching the numbers, I asked the essential question: What are you going to do with the rest of your life?

Some had well thought out plans. They wanted to do charity work or start a second career. Others didn't. Working at IBM was not just a job, it was a lifestyle. They had never thought about life outside the corporation.

IBM employees were like a large family. They had generous benefits and perks. Most socialized with other IBM employees. Once someone started at IBM, they generally stayed for life.

The idea of leaving IBM was painful.

Companies offering severance packages are generally established companies who sold the concept of lifetime employment concept. They are not places that fire employees without warning.

I've found that people leaving old line companies, even with a severance package, were bitterer than those where companies treated employees like interchangeable parts.

If you work at a company with high employee turnover, getting fired is not a total surprise. People at a company like IBM or Ford never thought about working somewhere else.

There are people who are married to their jobs. They don't have hobbies or outside interests. Those are people who need to forget about a severance package and stay put.

An engineer came to my office with many boxes of data (that he brought on a dolly). He had spent hours trying to quantify his decision. Before I went through his boxes, I asked some questions.

Did he like his job? Yes. Did they want him at the new company? Yes. Would he enjoy retirement? No. Could he find a similar job? Not in this part of the country. Was moving an option? No.

I told him to skip the number crunching. He needed to stay where he was. He was stunned. He wanted me to look at his boxes.

I wouldn't look at his data. I told him it was irrelevant. After a while, my words sunk in.

He worked happily for another decade.

Economic decisions shouldn't be ignored. Some severance packages are lucrative and offered on a one time basis. Financial considerations are one part of the package, not the whole package.

The health of the company and industry are important factors to consider.

I've seen people pass up a buyout and have their company go down a few years later. People often think their own industry is healthier than it is. It is good to get an objective opinion.

When auto workers were offered retirement incentives, I told most workers to take them. The older workers could guarantee health insurance and retirement income. The younger workers could maintain their lifestyle while they trained in another industry.

There are economic factors I look for in a plan. First is lifetime income. It's easier to leave if your lifetime income is secured. A second factor is health insurance. Larger companies have better benefits than what people can get on their own, especially if people have complicated medical conditions.

There have been calls for universal health care, but I wouldn't factor that into the decision. Don't make assessments based on things that may or may not happen.

I warn people getting lump sum packages not to make any sudden or stupid financial decisions. When severance plans are offered, I see hucksters come running, pitching everything from financial products to fast food franchises.

The best advice is to take a deep breath.

Talk, really talk, with your family, your bosses, your co-workers and the stakeholders in your decision. Get some outside and impartial advice. Make a decision based on information and logic, not on fear or emotion.

It's one of the most important decisions of your life. Even with good information, it is a decision you will ultimately make alone.

Mistakes with Children's Money
(2010)

"And here I sit so patiently
Waiting to find out what price
You have to pay to get out of
Going through all these things twice"
-Bob Dylan

I see people make the same mistakes over and over. This is particularly true when watching people handle money for children.

Terri Cullan, columnist for the *Wall Street Journal*, recently wrote about instructing children about money. The children Cullan wrote about come from families with lots of money. Cullan did not discuss a group I see frequently: children with money whose parents don't have much.

A number of children inherit money or receive money from an injury or other type of settlement. These children will often have a larger net worth than their parents.

This imbalance of wealth can cause family pressures. I've seen children try to use their wealth to belittle their poorer parents. I've seen parents succumb to temptation and use the child's money for themselves. In some cases, I have seen parents steal all of a child's money. If the parents have any money left, the child options are to prosecute or sue their parents to get the money back.

Not a great way to promote family unity.

Most states, including Kentucky, have guardianship laws set up to protect a child's money. These laws work when they are followed and enforced.

A flaw in guardianship laws is that most allow children to take control of the money on their 18th birthday and spend it as they wish.

Few 18-year-olds are prepared to handle a large lump sum of money. Laws prevent people from buying alcohol until age 21. However, it is assumed that people who can't legally buy a beer can somehow be responsible for handling thousands and sometimes millions of dollars.

There are some simple financial planning techniques to keep a child from getting all the money at age 18. I urge parents and guardians to use these concepts, but many do not.

I have seen case after case where guardians turn all the money over to the child on the 18th birthday. I hate it. It is like watching a train wreck over and over again and not being able to stop it.

Many 18-year-olds feel pressured to spend money on their friends. The child with the lump sum will be the most popular in the neighborhood until the money runs out.

Eighteen-year-olds with lots of cash are good for car dealers, people who sell liquor and oftentimes drug dealers. I know there are some 18-year-olds who handle money well, but for over 20 years, I have watched many 18-year-olds run through their money in no time.

One of the worst cases I've been involved in was when I could not convince a parent to defer a lump sum over a series of years. Instead the money was put in a bank account and $100,000 was given to the young man on his 18th birthday. He used the money to develop a cocaine habit and when that money ran out, he shot a man while trying to rob a pool hall. One man is dead and another in prison the rest of his life because an 18-year-old got too much money at once.

I blame the parents and guardians for putting the 18-year-old in a disastrous position. Many young people who blew their money look back later and wish they had a second chance to do it right.

I read that a person's financial profile is set at age 27. If someone is a spender before age 27, they might turn it around later. If they are a spender after age 27, they will be that way the rest of their lives.

Twenty-seven may not be the magic age of financial fate, but that is a time when many people are starting their careers and starting a family. They will make more mature decisions than they would at age 18.

The best idea is to give children a chance to have some money available when they are older and can make better decisions.

Friends and Your Money: Hanging onto Both of Them
(2012)

Being taken by those supposedly close to someone with money is a universal problem.

I know many people of extreme wealth, and many keep it by constantly mistrusting those around them. Living life in constant suspicion of your family and friends doesn't sound like fun.

Some simple rules for friendship need to prevail:

1. Never lend money to anyone. You are a person, not a bank.

Follow the advice of William Shakespeare. In *Hamlet*, Lord Polonius said, "Neither a borrower nor a lender be; For loan oft loses both itself and friend, And borrowing dulls the edge of husbandry."

In modern terms, "Friends don't borrow money from friends. That is what banks are for."

In a world of banks, automobile financing, mortgage brokers, credit cards, payday lenders, pawn shops and "buy here/pay here" car lots, someone intent on borrowing money can find a professional lender willing to give them money at a rate suitable to their credit history.

They don't need to borrow from their friends.

Most of the time, the friend subconsciously (or even consciously) considers the loan a "gift" and, as Shakespeare noted, it usually ends the friendship.

Like most people, I've been burned on lending money. The last person I lent money to (several years ago) was a very close friend who makes big money. This person also had big issues I did not know about. I lent an amount I could afford. I thought it was on a short-term basis. I've never seen a dime in repayment and rarely see the friend anymore.

We all make that mistake once or twice in our lives. Anyone who has not done it, please jump up and do a cartwheel. You are a distinct minority.

The key is to learn from mistakes. I did. I don't lend money to anyone. I don't cosign either. My children have a similar philosophy.

People will make you think you are a jerk when you turn them down. Actually the opposite is true. Not lending money is more likely to prolong a friendship than lending it.

2. If someone needs an expensive gift to be your friend, they are not actually your friend.

I felt sorry for Michael Jackson. He was a star from early childhood and never got to meet normal people. He was always surrounded by a large entourage, but always had to pay for them to go places. Or pay them a salary.

I have friends in all walks of life. Some possess genius level IQ's and some don't. Some are multimillionaires and some have to save up to go to lunch at a fast food restaurant. The key is that, for whatever reason, we enjoy each other's company.

It can be tough for people with money to make friends. Like the Eagles song "Lyin' Eyes" says, "a big old house can get lonely," and having money as a measure of control makes it tempting for wealthy people to "buy" people to hang out with.

On the other hand, if you have to buy your friends, you are getting what you pay for. Life is better when you find real people who want your company and not your wallet.

3. If you like hanging out with wealthy people, pick up the check when you dine with them.

My father made good money, but when he died in 1993, he was not a man of great wealth. The average net worth of his pallbearers went well into the millions. Dad's close friend, Hall of Fame disc jockey Jim LaBarbara, said that "Big Joe McNay was bigger than life. He was friends with everyone from (Johnny) Bench and Pete (Rose) to the big politicians. I think he introduced me to half the people in town (Cincinnati), everyone seemed to like him."

Dad was always the first to grab a check and never forgot his friends' birthdays. Many people expect to be "treated" when they are dining with a wealthy person. I've actually seen people order the most expensive things on a menu when they think someone with more income is paying. It's amazing how some can have "short arm disease" when the check arrives.

Dad was the opposite. He found that wealth was one byproduct for people living interesting lives. He was glad to pick up the tab to be in their inner circle. He was the kind of friend a wealthy person wants to have. Thus, his world was filled with them.

4. Friendship is a lifelong journey, not a drive-by experience.

My book is dedicated to my grandson and my friends who stood up for me at my wedding. The men have all had successful careers and are wonderful role models for children. They have also been my friends for many decades. Even if I don't talk to them for months, I always feel a deep connection.

I am confident that if I won the lottery, none of them would be looking for a handout. All of them would be happy for me. Just like I would be for them.

I meet people who seem to trade in their friends for a new group every year or so. They try to be with the "in crowd" or never get too deep into getting to know someone.

All relationships require trust, love, giving, commitment and flexibility. People who have totally invested in their relationships are less likely to fall prey to an "entourage" or "posse" wanting their money.

Since family and friends are the primary reasons that people blow a lump sum, if you can invest in good quality relationships, you can go a long way toward maintaining financial success as well.

Good Deals with Bad People
(2007)

"If his lips are moving, he's lying"
-D'Ramirez

There are some people you do business with and others you don't.
Wayne Rogers had a simple way of ferreting them out.

Rogers, best known as Trapper John on the television show
*M*A*S*H*, had a second career as an investment and business guru.

According to Rogers, there are four kinds of business deals: good
deals with good people, bad deals with bad people, good deals with
bad people and bad deals with good people.

The first two are simple. Everyone wants good deals with good
people, and no one wants bad deals with bad people.

Regarding the other possibilities, Rogers said that good deals with
bad people will always fail and that a bad deal with good people
could potentially work out someday.

A bad person will always make a good deal go bad, and a good
person might make a bad deal right.

Character is more important than talent, a great deal or promised
riches.

It is surprising how many businesses don't get it. Some sports teams
don't get it either.

The Cincinnati Bengals should be headed for the Super Bowl.
Instead, they are watching the playoffs on television. They have a
talented football team. They also are making a lot of lawyers and
bail bondmen rich. It seemed like every week during the season, a
Bengal did something stupid or criminal—often both.

The team had several players you would never invite over for dinner. Unless you had armed guards around the house.

The Bengals lost five games that they should have won. A team with more character would have pulled a few out.

Paul Brown, who founded the Bengals, was a believer in hiring well-rounded players.

When all-pro defensive tackle Mike Reid quit to become a musician, Brown encouraged him to pursue his dream. I don't know if Brown was alive when Reid started receiving Grammy awards, but he would have been proud. Brown had character and looked for players who mirrored his values.

As a longsuffering Bengals fan, I am frustrated by the choices that the team's management has made.

Because they live their lives in the public eye, it is easy to spot character, determination and team spirit in professional athletes. It is a lot harder to spot those traits in businesspeople.

Like everyone in business, I've been burned by bad people that I thought were good. However, I have not been burned chasing deals with people I don't trust. I know that there is no such thing as a good deal with a bad person.

Even before Wayne Rogers summed it up, I watched my late father do business as a gambler. In his era, you couldn't sue to enforce a gambling debt. All that Dad had was a person's word that they were good for the money.

It worked for him. In a world where trust was everything, a person's reputation became known quickly.

His philosophy was "don't do business with scum balls."

It seems like an easy lesson that some people don't get.

I've had people tell me about deals that are good to be true. It was because they weren't true. The people peddling them had no history of ever telling the truth. I heard my dad tell a man once, "I judge horses on past performance, and based on your past performance, you are never getting money from me."

It is not that hard to figure out who is good and who is bad. Some people will fool you, but if you do some homework and be realistic in your expectations, you will rarely get burned.

The Bengals weren't realistic in what they expected. They expected players who know the jailer on a first-name basis to develop character and a winning attitude.

If a football player or a businessperson has a history of being a troublemaker, they will be a cancer to those around them. They will bring the good players down to their level.

I hope the Bengals get rid of the troublemakers. If nothing else, it will cut down on their legal expenses. Like in business, they should realize that when faced with a "great deal" from someone with a dubious reputation, just keep singing, "If their lips are moving, they are lying."

The "Trailer Park Test"
(2012)

"Yeah life here in the trailer park is fine,
You know that we've been living it every day
I got me a good looking woman
I got me some indoor plumbing
And I wouldn't have it any other way"
-Pat Green

My daughter, Angela Luhys, developed a concept that she called the "trailer park test."

When a man tried to impress her with material possessions, she always imagined if she would still like him if he lived in a trailer park instead of a nice house.

If she decided that she would still like the guy if he lived in a trailer park, he stayed. If she decided that his money played into how she viewed him, he went.

Not a bad system.

Angela, who wants (and deserves) full and total credit for coining the phrase "trailer park test," works with me at the McNay Group, where we deal with injured people, lottery winners and others who come into sudden money.

We realized that the "trailer park test" is not just a dating tool; it is a way to measure how people interact with anyone with money.

You frequently see professional athletes and lottery winners develop a group called "the posse." In Elvis's case, it was called the Memphis Mafia. The posse is a group of hangers-on who tell the wealthy person what they want to hear and hope to have money and reflected glory.

The posse is also the reason that an estimated 90 percent of lottery winners and the majority of professional athletes are broke within five years of earning their money.

The person who gets a large sum of money should do a "reverse trailer park test" on their potential posse. Ask themselves if the "friends" or new "romantic interest" would still be in their life if they lived in a trailer park.

Probably not.

Some people have a healthy relationship with money. They view it as a tool to provide for themselves and their families and live a comfortable life. They are not interested, like Will Rogers used to say, "in spending money they don't have to impress people they don't know."

Recently, an accomplished professional woman told me she had wanted to marry a rich man at one point in her life.

My response was why?

She makes a high income and made the money herself. She put herself through years of school doing menial jobs and has a strong sense of independence. She has a balanced life, no material needs or wants and no desire to show off.

I told her that she would never give up her independence for any amount of money. The money would make her less happy, not more.

She would rather live in a trailer park with someone she loves than a mansion with someone who brought angst, unhappiness and complication.

Angela is hoping that the "trailer park test" becomes a national standard on how people relate to those who have more income or possessions than they do.

It won't solve all the world's problems, but the "trailer park test" is a pretty good place to start.

Bait and Switch Business Relationships
(2009)

"All of this, all of this, all of this looks so easy"
But all of this, all of this, all of this ain't so easy"
-Saliva

Entrepreneur coach Dan Sullivan spoke at the Million Dollar Round Table International meeting a few weeks ago. Sullivan said that entrepreneurs often neglected people who were their best clients.

He compared it to marriage. He said that when people are in a courtship, no one is ever "too busy." Once they get married, the spouse is often secondary to factors like work, family and other interests.

Sullivan said that many spouses could be accused of "bait and switch." They were sold one type of relationship and got another.

The same hold true for many business clients.

Sullivan, "The Strategic Coach," is one of the most important influences in my life. I spent a year going to Toronto to take his classes and the experience was life-changing. I thought I knew everything he had to say, but when he used the "bait and switch" line, it was like a punch to the gut.

It made me realize what many of us do, in business and life. We overlook the people who are closest to us.

My structured settlement firm was built by attorneys and claims people referring clients to me. Business doesn't come from any other source. Most have been sending clients for over 20 years and are intensely loyal. When they quit referring me and start using a competitor, it hurts. It REALLY hurts. It is like losing a family member.

It doesn't happen often, but it happens. When I find out why, it is almost universally the same answer:

Someone else took the time to build a closer relationship.

It is never about competence or job performance, it is always about relationship. Sometimes the competitor has a geographic or family connection, but sometimes it is because the referral source has not seen me in a long time.

Sullivan has you list your top 20 clients. When you go down the list and note the last time you have seen them in person, it can be an eye-opening experience.

Email, texting and sending a monthy newsletter doesn't count. To keep a relationship, you have to spend time with them.

Dan Sullivan noted that the "bait and switch" trait was one that many entrepreneurs shared. Especially those who experienced rapid growth and success. The business owner is so focused on a higher goal that they forget about the people who help get them there.

Malcolm Gladstone wrote an outstanding book called *The Tipping Point* and discussed people called "connectors." Connectors go out of their way to refer people to other people.

I'm that kind of guy. If I like a service, person or product, I tell everyone about it. I have a wide social network and plenty of life experiences. If you want a left-handed bricklayer in Cincinnati, I can find you one. (In fact, I know two of them.) About 20 years ago, one of Al Gore's close friends needed a dentist for his daughter at midnight. I found the right person within 15 minutes.

I give more restaurant reviews than Zagat. We just eat in a different style of restaurant.

I may be good, but I have friends who are better. In our little network, we can find experts at everything.

How and why a person refers tells a lot about character. Often times, people will use a referral question as a way to find employment for an idiot brother-in-law. They aren't interested in helping a person solve a problem; they are trying to steer income to a buddy.

When I find a person like that, they are never going to get a referral from me. I ultimately can't trust their judgment or motives.

I want my referer to send the best person for a job, not a person who needs a job the most.

When people get to the top and dominate their profession, they assume that potential customers will come to them because they are the best. Thus, they leave themselves vulnerable to someone who is developing relationships at other levels.

Mark McCormick, who founded the IMG sports marketing empire, gave a great example in his book, *What They Don't Teach You at Harvard Business School*. McCormick's first three clients were Arnold Palmer, Jack Nickalas and Gary Player, the three greatest golfers of that generation.

He naturally assumed that all other golfers would come to him and his lack of a "courtship" allowed competitors to spring up and pick off business.

McCormick and IMG figured out their mistake. Tiger Woods is one of IMG's current clients. They started their courtship of Tiger early on and I am sure of one thing.

You will never hear Tiger complaining about IMG giving him a "bait and switch" relationship.

Money and the Marshmallow
(2009)

"Well, the devil made me do it the first time
The second time I done it on my own"
-Billy Joe Shaver

The New Yorker published a 2009 story about the psychology of delayed gratification.

It discussed a group of four-year-old nursery school students who were part of a study done at Stanford University in the late 1960s.

The children were given the opportunity to eat a marshmallow. Ones who ate it immediately only received one marshmallow. The ones who waited for an undetermined time (up to 15 minutes) would receive a second marshmallow.

Most of the children couldn't wait. Most grabbed and ate the first marshmallow immediately.

The psychologist tracked the participants over the next 40 years. The children who waited for the second marshmallow went on to live productive, and in many cases, outstanding lives.

Those who immediately grabbed a marshmallow didn't do as well.

Walter Mischel, the Stanford psychology professor who did the study, got serious about tracking the students in 1981. He studied every trait he could think of.

The students who couldn't wait were more prone to adult behavior problems and inability to deal with stress.

When they got to college age, the nursery school students who waited 15 minutes averaged SAT scores 215 points higher than those who could only wait 30 seconds.

Mischel seems to have discovered the Rosetta Stone of why some people become wealthy and others do not.

Dr. Thomas Stanley has done extensive research into why some people become millionaires. His book, *The Millionaire Next Door,* was a huge bestseller.

Stanley noted that education and intelligence did not automatically predict wealth. He said that small business owners, without advanced degrees, were more likely to be millionaires than were doctors or lawyers.

I've been in the financial services business all of my adult life, and it has always amazed me how some well-educated people make such stupid mistakes with their money.

Now I understand. The doctors and lawyers were the people who couldn't wait for the marshmallow.

The Stanford scientists are studying genetics and are trying to learn if some regions of the brain assist in delaying gratification. The study gives credence to the idea that people who "can't help themselves" really can't help themselves. Something in their DNA makes it harder for some people to delay getting a reward.

It's not about discipline as much as it is about heredity. Knowing that, we need to help those who are prone to marshmallow grabbing by giving them fewer chances to fail.

Right now, we have a financial system that has played to people's weaknesses, rather than their strengths.

We have allowed people who are prone to instant gratification to have as much credit as they could get their hands on. College students were given credit cards and free t-shirts. People who didn't want to save for a down payment were given sub-prime mortgages. Payday lenders popped up to prey upon the poorest of the poor, who couldn't wait for their paychecks. Everyone and everything (including dogs, cats and dead people) have been issued credit cards.

We stopped giving workers defined-benefit pensions and let them "pick their own investments" in 401(k) plans.

The economy is a mess. That mess can be traced to people on Wall Street and Main Street who wanted the second marshmallow, but didn't want to wait for it.

Now that we are starting to understand the problem, it is easier to find solutions. We need systems that encourage people and businesses to work toward long-term rewards.

Our leaders need to realize that a large segment of society is going to screw-up their finances if we let them.

We can't let what has happened, happen again.

The devil, their environment or genetics caused people to make mistakes the first time.

It is our job to make sure they can't do it a second time.

Section Two

Anna Nicole and Dying Rich
(2007)

"Get rich or die trying"
-50 Cent

I just watched the movie, *Get Rich or Die Trying*. The main character was a fascinating study of someone who viewed money and status as the key to happiness.

Being rich doesn't make you happy. Ask anyone who knew Anna Nicole Smith if you need more elaboration.

The saddest are those who get rich through lottery, inheritance or some other one time money, and then blow it.

They had a chance, but couldn't make it work.

It's been said that 90 percent of people who receive a lump sum of money will run through it all in five years or less. After 24 years of doing financial counseling for lottery winners and injured people, I am sure that that figure is correct.

It overwhelms most people to receive a large lump sum of money. They make mistakes and let people take advantage of them.

Some people view the wasted lives of lottery winners as proof that money is evil.

Money isn't evil. Even quick money is not evil. Money allows us to feed our families and live a high-quality lifestyle. It is the exchange system we use to translate work product into rewards.

Get rich or die trying is not a motto to many people; it is a lifestyle. Like sex, drugs and rock-and-roll, money can become an obsession.

Just watching people with money, like Anna Nicole or Paris Hilton, has become important to some people.

It is said that money is the root of all evil. A television minister named Reverend Ike said that the lack of money is the root of all evil.

I say that the lack of respect for money is really the root of all evil.

I've dealt with over 2,000 people have come into instant money either through a settlement or a lottery. The people that set financial limits and goals live happily. Those without limits often end up making a fool out of themselves.

The unhappy people did not have respect for the money. Money is like fire or a dangerous substance. You have to understand that it can do good and evil.

If, after receiving a lump sum of money, you take 50 of your closest "friends" to the Super Bowl, you don't have respect for the money. If you go into a strip joint with $600,000 in cash, like Powerball winner Jack Whittaker did, you don't have respect for the money.

Most people have friends within 15 percent of their own income class. When someone wealthy has friends who are poor, it is hard for them to do the same things socially.

Some big spenders think that money can buy them love, friends or happiness.

What kind of person would want "love" from someone who wants them only for their money?

It would be a lot cheaper and productive to dump the "friend" and spend the money on a good therapist.

There is not a law against being stupid. When a 60-year-old lottery winner suddenly gets an 18-year-old lover, the lover is not with them for their looks.

I really don't understand the inner mind of people who leech. They are certainly out there. Look at the big "posse" that lottery winners have.

How much self-respect can a person like that have? I wonder how people get up in the morning knowing that they are going to suck money from someone who trusts them.

People who earn money learn to respect its power. You don't see many self-made millionaires doing the stupid things that lottery winners are known for.

Go to a self-made person and see if they are paying people to be their friends. It does not happen. The self-made person has sweat and stress invested in the creation of money.

They view their money with proper respect.

There has been too much media coverage of Anna Nicole. She did not earn her wealth or make the world a better place. Her big accomplishment was inheriting money.

She managed to be rich and die trying.

How Do I Live Without You?
(2005)

"How do I live without you? I want to know
How do I breathe without you?
If you ever go, how do I ever, ever survive?
O how do I live?"
-Trisha Yearwood

Kathy Trant attracted worldwide attention by saying she has spent most of the $4.7 million she received for the death of her husband who was killed in the September 11, 2001 World Trade Center attack.

I'm not surprised about Trant's story. I've seen the same story played out hundreds of times with larger and smaller sums of money.

I've spent nearly 24 years giving financial advice to the families of people who were killed.

Trant called the money "blood money." Her spending sprees are a subconscious or conscious effort to run through the money.

It is a common feeling amongst widows and widowers.

Shopping and spending can be an escape and people will keep spending money to find relief from their pain.

Some people use drugs and alcohol. These people use "blood money".

Many people think that if they get rid of the money their lives will go back to normal.

Often, I see a grief-ridden person influenced by family and friends. The person will turn over their money to a third party and let that person make all the financial decisions.

I've had a number of widowers and widows remarry quickly and then turn all financial decisions over to the new spouse. Usually, the new spouse and the money run out at about the same time.

Twenty years ago, I had a client whose wife was killed in a car wreck. He agreed to a structured settlement for his children's money, but wanted his $500,000 "liquid." Within three months of his first wife's death, he had remarried.

He was a roofer who lived simply. His new wife handled the finances.

I invested his money, but every month, the new wife would come to my office wanting to withdraw more. Each time, she was sporting new jewelry, a mink coat and other expensive items. I finally went to their house and told them they were going to run out of money. She got mad and he tuned me out. They moved their money to another broker.

Six months later, his lawyer told me that she had spent the entire $500,000 and left town.

I heard from the roofer last year. His children, who were infants when we met, had both graduated from college and he thanked me for putting their money away where his ex-wife could not touch it.

Putting money in a structured settlement and paying it out monthly is the only real solution I have. I don't know if Kathy Trant was offered a structured settlement, but doubt she was. Most of the families of September 11 victims were offered cash only. That was a really dumb decision. You will be hearing more stories like Kathy Trant's soon.

I started out using structured settlements as a financial planning tool and became a true believer. About 10 years ago, I quit offering investments like stocks, bonds and mutual funds. Hurting people need the stability and regular payments that a structured settlement offers.

It is hard for someone who has gone through hell to think clearly about their money. Someone who has just lost their spouse has no chance.

There is a small window of time before people actually receive money to set things up right. After that, pressures and people get in the way.

I feel sorry for everyone involved. I feel sorry for the widows and widowers. Not only have they lost their spouses, after they run through the money they are worse off financially than ever.

Also, I feel bad about the spouses who died thinking that their families were taken care of. People buy life insurance because they want their loved ones to achieve life goals. They don't pay for life insurance so that someone can take 30 "friends" to the Super Bowl or so a new spouse can buy a Rolex.

I set up the finances for a woman who knew she was dying. We assured that her husband, daughter, grandson and church would receive regular lifetime payments. We left a large sum available for her while she was alive. She did not live to spend it and her husband spent it wisely in the first years after her death. Now he has a new wife and they are taking the money in huge chunks. When the lump sum is gone, he will still have the monthly payments.

A lot of widow and widowers wake up every day asking "how can I live without you?" I'm not sure how, but they eventually start to cope with their situation.

Kathy Trant has been through hell. If her attorneys, advisors or friends had insisted that she needed to put her money in a structured settlement or a trust, she would be able to live a comfortable life.

Now she won't. She can't get the money back from the 30 leaches that she took to the Super Bowl (people who prey on grieving widows don't have the money or conscience to help her) and she still thinks that getting rid of the money will somehow bring back her husband and her old life.

Her husband is not coming back. She and others like her need to answer the question, "how do I live without you?" by answering, "with great memories and the money you left to help me through this."

College Graduation: A Very Special Mother's Day Gift

(2011)

"And with the power of conviction
There is no sacrifice
It's a do or die situation
We will be invincible"
-Pat Benatar

Several years back, Sunday, May 8 was Mother's Day. It was also graduation day at Northern Kentucky University.

I was at Northern, watching my nephew, Nick McNay, go through the graduation procession.

His grandmother, Ollie, and mother, Theresa, were watching from a perch up in the heavens.

Graduating from college was something that Nick did to honor them. Going on to live an educated and productive life is something he will do for himself and his children.

His journey is one of inspiration and perseverance.

Few things in Nick's early environment predicted that someday he would be on the Dean's List and walking down a college graduation line.

He was the son of a single mother and has met his father once. College is not a family tradition. He and I, exactly 30 years apart, are the only McNay's ever to graduate from college.

His high school did not produce many college graduates. Nick spent most of high school playing basketball and soccer and chasing girls.

Although he excelled at all three, they were not predictors of future academic success.

He had some things going for him. With a charming personality, strong work ethic and street smarts, he has always been a natural leader.

After high school, he bounced through a series of manual labor jobs and didn't have a plan or direction.

That all changed on April 2, 2006. The day his grandmother, Ollie, died.

Ollie came back from a party, complained of a headache and suddenly died right in front of Nick and his mother. She had an aneurysm.

Nick wrote in a college paper, "My grandma was more to me than just a grandma. She was my father, best friend, biggest supporter, lifeline; words can't express what she was to me. All she ever asked me to do was to go to college."

He decided that day to get his college degree. He came to Richmond, Kentucky to attend my alma mater, Eastern Kentucky University.

He went at his classes with intensity and enthusiasm. He didn't have a major, but he was motivated to fulfill the college dreams his grandmother had for him.

Then the second blow struck. Six months after his grandmother died, his mother, who had just found a great job at Proctor and Gamble, fell down a flight of steps and died at age 46. Both of his parental figures were gone.

It would have been easy to give up and quit.

Instead, he "doubled down," to use a gambling expression.

Nick became even more focused on school to help block out his grief. He also went to weekly counseling sessions, found an army of tutors and used every support resource that EKU had to offer.

The person who really helped to pull him through was his math teacher. The teacher spent many after class hours helping him understand math and also counseling him with his problems.
I found out two years later that the math teacher was Robert Blythe, who is also a minister and Richmond City Commissioner.

Nick made it through the year and studied in Brazil that summer.

That fall, he fathered a child in Cincinnati—another reason to drop out of school. Instead, Nick doubled down again.

He transferred to Northern Kentucky University to be near the first of his two daughters, working at cutting down trees and delivering pizzas while he attended class.

At Northern, he found his calling. The school has an excellent program in Electronic Media Broadcasting in the College of Informatics. Once Nick took an introductory class, he was hooked. The formerly indifferent student started showing up on the Dean's List with a passion and enthusiasm for cinematography.

Nick did an internship for Above the Line Media in Cincinnati and worked directly with its president, award-winning filmmaker Mark Turner. (In an ironic twist, Turner was the editor of my college newspaper.) Turner had just finished work on *4192*, a documentary about Pete Rose.

Turner said, "Nick has a very good eye for framing a shot. I trusted him with shots that are going to show up at film festivals and on DVD. As good as his instincts are now, they are only going to get better. He has a bright future in this business."

In days when college tuition is spiraling and people like Mark Zuckerberg and Bill Gates are making billions without a diploma, some argue that a college degree may not be worth the expense.

When I ponder the cost versus the benefit, I look at the situations of people like Nick. College gave Nick a framework to utilize his intellect and discover gifts that he never knew he had.

Instead of a lifetime of going from one manual labor job to another, he had a start at a high-powered career that he absolutely loved.

Pressure is what turns a piece of coal into a diamond. The pressures Nick had to overcome allowed his talents, work ethic and character to flourish.

His grandmother and mother knew that Nick was a "diamond in the rough" and that college would smooth out the rough edges.

On that Mother's Day, they got to see their dreams and wishes come true.

From a perch above the clouds.

Section Three

SEND LAWYERS GUNS AND MONEY

Why Mitt Romney Should Proudly Release His Tax Returns
(2012)

One of the first things that I tell lottery winners or those who come into big money is to find a top notch team of advisors. My rule of thumb is to find someone who has handled more money than what you are bringing them.

That is exactly what Mitt Romney did.

As far as I can tell, Romney has not committed any crimes. He has not evaded taxes or used illegal tax shelters.

He used the tax advantages that Congress granted him and many other wealthy people.

Wealthy people can afford to hire big time lobbyists and raise tons of money for political campaigns.

Average Americans can't. Thus, the rich people get their way in Washington.

We have wound up with a mish mash of laws that favor the wealthy.

The laws favor certain classes of people more than others.

If someone receives money in a punitive damages lawsuit, the money is fully taxable. If they are a Wall Street hedge fund manager, gains are often taxed in a lower bracket.

The middle class get hit the worst. If a coal miner loses his job and cashes in his retirement or 401k account to feed his family, he pays ordinary income taxes and a ten percent tax penalty to boot.

Jimmy Carter once said, "Life isn't fair," and there is nothing fair about the tax code.

This brings us to the Mitt Romney situation.

Romney has made a ton of money. He has not released all of his tax returns and keeps hoping that people will leave him alone and forget about them. They won't.

Americans want their leaders to come clean and not appear to be hiding something.

The worst thing Romney can do politically is to keep stalling. It allows Obama to be on the offensive instead of forced to defend his record in office.

There will be a day when Romney does get pressured into releasing his taxes.

When he does, we will probably find a lot of loopholes, offshore accounts and plenty of ways that Mitt has reduced his taxable income from some insanely high number to something more manageable.

To the point where he is probably in a lower bracket than Warren Buffett's secretary.

Is that Mitt's fault or Congress's fault?

If I had Mitt's money, I would be looking for every tax advantage that Congress has to offer.

If I were a financial adviser to Mitt Romney, I would be helping him find those tax advantages. Just like any other good adviser would do.

Next month will mark my 30th year in the financial business. I've yet to find someone who didn't take a tax break, like deducting the interest on their mortgage, when that tax break was legal and available.

You can't fault Mitt for doing what the rest of us do. He has more money so he found more complicated ways to shelter income.

Congress, not Mitt, allowed those breaks.

I'm a lifelong Democrat who voted for Obama in 2008, but I truly see Mitt's political dilemma.

If he releases his returns, people are going to see deductions, loopholes and tax shelters that average Americans are not in a position to take advantage of.

If he doesn't release the returns, people are going to assume he did something crooked.

One of the advantages that Romney has is that people seem to think he is an honest, family-oriented man.

Goofy, ill at ease, and clueless about how average Americans live their lives, but many people trust Romney.

That trust starts eroding each day the tax returns don't get released.

Romney has a chance to spin the issue his way. Courtesy of Romney's former arch nemesis, Mike Huckabee.

Huckabee ran for President in 2008 on a consumption tax, called the FAIR tax, which also allowed credits for people with lower income. It eliminated almost all deductions and Huckabee claimed it would eliminate the IRS.

Embracing the FAIR plan could make Romney president.

It would help Romney with Tea Party members who don't trust him and give Romney an issue that would force Obama to explain why he has not closed the loopholes.

It allows Romney to take a negative and make it a positive. It also keeps him on the offensive.

Duck and run is not what people want to see in a President.

People know the tax system is out of whack and unfair. It is by the rich, for the rich, to help the rich.

A FAIR tax might level the playing field. Especially if it is advocated by a multimillionaire with a Swiss bank account.

Small Town Values in Big Time Lawyer
(2009)

"Yeah, I can be myself here in this small town
And people let me be just what I want to be"
- John Mellencamp

For all my adult life, I've assisted trial attorneys with structured settlements. I've worked with big names in big cities, but the best seem to come from small towns.

Like James (J.T) Gilbert, in my hometown of Richmond, Kentucky.

J.T. is the kind of lawyer every small town should have. He spent 18 years as Chair of the Board of Regents at Eastern Kentucky University and longer as city attorney for the neighboring city of Berea.

Along the way, he became one of the nation's top trial lawyers.

He is President-elect of the Kentucky Justice Association. Next week, in Boston, he will be inducted into the American College of Trial Lawyers.

The American College of Trial Lawyers is a big time deal. Its membership can never be more than one percent of the attorneys in any state or province.

Its membership includes big stars and big hitters. And a small town lawyer from Kentucky.

Kentucky has its share of big time rural lawyers. Sam Davies in Barbourville and Richard Hay in Somerset are two of the best injury attorneys the nation has ever produced.

The big cities and their big populations are well represented, but it's easy to see why small town lawyers make it to the top.

It's like Mr. Mellencamp said, "People in small towns can be who they want to be."

There is a feeling of grounding that helps develop the skills to be a top notch trial lawyer.

Small town juries won't allow you to pull the stunts that you see on *Boston Legal* or in the O.J. Simpson trial. They won't tolerate a lot of flash and showboating.

Depending on your perspective, there is a good and bad to small towns. Everyone knows everything about everybody. It's like a scaled down version of Facebook expect you don't get to choose the news that is posted.

Outside of President Obama and Theodore Roosevelt, almost all United States presidents grew up in small towns. I don't think that is accident. Small communities develop a sense of service and a work ethic that people distant from their neighbors don't have.

Small town values can exists in any geographic area. People from places like Brooklyn and the south side of Chicago often have the sense of community that small town Kentuckians have.

It could be that President Obama is a small town guy after all. The South Side gave him that sense of belonging.

I might be making too much of the big town/small town thing. I've spent most of my life dealing with Wall Street types and I'm often the only small town person in the room.

I've gotten remarks about my accent and whether I grew up with running water. (I grew up in a Cincinnati suburb with an in-ground swimming pool in the backyard.)

There are three ways to react to snobbery. One is to feel inferior. The second is to rise above it and outperform the people putting you down. The third is to just ignore it and live your life the way you want to live it.

I think J.T. Gilbert took the third route. He goes at life with the determination to make a difference. He's also just a genuinely nice guy. You want him to be your neighbor and I was in a sense. For seven years, I rented the office building next to his law firm.

I could talk to him on a regular basis and appreciated his reasoning and insights. I trusted him to be the executor for my will.

My family knows if I drop over tomorrow to get ahold of J.T. and start making arrangements.

Like John Mellencamp, I'll probably die in a small town and probably where they will bury me.

Guys like J.T. Gilbert are the reason I stay here.

Macho Man Ralph Nader
(2008)

"Call him Mr. Ego
He's a Macho Man"
-Village People

I never believed when that song came out that someday I would be using it to describe Ralph Nader.

Ralph Nader was one of my childhood heroes. I read all of his books, stood in line to meet him and tried to get a job with his organization. Ralph Nader was the kind of American I wanted to be.

These days I would have a hard time being in same room with him. Ralph's need to feed his ego hurt the cause that he spent his life fighting for. His run for President in 2000 was driven by his inner need to be seen as macho, tough and relevant.

I worked for Al Gore's first presidential campaign in 1988 and wanted him to win in 2000. A lot of factors played into Gore's loss, but Nader was the deciding factor.

Nader's push for consumer protection and product safety in the 1960s came when he was a young man. He received enormous amounts of publicity as his cause took hold. He was considered one of the most admired men in America.

As he got older, Ralph Nader did not make the headlines as often. Part of the reason was a shift in the country's values, but the main reason was that Ralph had been tremendously successful in what he set out to do. A whole generation of talented trial attorneys grew up doing battle with car manufacturers that compromised safety for quick profits because of Nader's investigations.

Ralph was not as "hot" as he was in the 1960s. He did not appear on the talk shows or host *Saturday Night Live* like he used to do.

When Madonna went through a career slump, she put out a book showing pictures of her having sex with Vanilla Ice. Michael Jackson kept the media on him by having plastic surgery and Britney Spears got married.

Plastic surgery, marriage or having sex with Vanilla Ice were all viable options for Ralph, but he chose to run for President instead.

Having high name recognition and some real accomplishments in the distant past, Ralph made an attractive candidate for about two percent of the voters.

In a landslide year, no one would care about Nader or other fringe candidates. In an election where one candidate won the popular vote and the other was given the electoral vote by the Supreme Court, it became obvious a few weeks out that Ralph's followers might make the difference.

Ralph acted like a teenager on a first date. He shoved his face on every television camera from the networks to the public access channel. Someone was paying attention to Ralph Nader again and he was going to suck up every minute of it.

The Ralph Nader that I always believed in would have recognized that Al Gore held the same ideals that he advocated and could do something about it. He would have understood that the cause was more important than his ego and stepped aside in favor of Gore.

Not this guy. Ralph recognized that the only way to keep the cameras on him was show that he was a macho man and hang in the race, no matter how much pressure was put on him. Ralph was going to recapture his fame once and for all. The country be dammed, Ralph needed his ego stroked.

I'm not sure he got what he wanted. After his flurry of media ended, he went back to being a has been. No one buys his books or listens to his speeches. He made some noise lately about running for President, but no one really cares.

Before he got lost in his ego, Ralph was a man with real values. You can't say that now, and it is really sad.

The irony is that the song "Macho Man" by the Village People is probably better known by the public than Ralph Nader is now.

If Ralph had really wanted to get noticed, he should have dressed up like a policeman, construction worker or cowboy and sung with the group.

He would have been happier and the country a lot better off.

Why Did Paula Deen's Legal Team Let Her Testify?
(2013)

"Everybody's got a secret sonny
Yeah, something that they just can't face
Some folks spend their whole lives trying to keep it
They carry it with them every step that they take"
-Bruce Springsteen

I can't imagine that Paula Deen and her legal team were blindsided by the line of questioning from Lisa Jackson's lawyer.

Jackson is suing Deen and her brother Bubba for creating a hostile work environment. In her amended complaint to file the lawsuit, Jackson said that she had suffered from "violent, sexist and racist behavior." It alleged that "racially discriminatory attitudes" were present. Although the allegations were primarily aimed at Bubba, it noted that "Paula Deen holds such racist views herself."

Paula's legal team flunked Risk Management 101. When they allowed Paula to give her deposition, they had to realize that the testimony would not be limited to her recipe for peanut butter pie.

The deposition process allowed the ugliest allegations to get on the record and in the public domain. They destroyed Paula's multimillion dollar business empire.

All from a lawsuit that should have been settled.

As a settlement planner and licensed claims adjuster, I've been involved in thousands of legal negotiations.

From a risk management standpoint, the Deen lawsuit was a no brainer. The worst Paula and her insurance carrier could lose was $1.2 million. Paula has that in her hip pocket.

Paula's team should have made the lawsuit go away quietly.

If I had been on Paula's risk management team, I would have asked Paula to have a settlement conference with Jackson. I also would have told Paula to:

1. Bring her checkbook.

2. Apologize sincerely and profusely.

3. Make sure that the settlement agreement has a strong confidentiality clause so the settlement or anything said does not make it into the public domain.

Settling claims is about risk management. Risk management is a lot like my late father's career as a bookie and professional gambler.

The key to bookmaking is not to hit a big jackpot. It is to minimize your losses.

Settling insurance claims works the same way. You have to look at what an ugly lawsuit will do to your overall reputation and business and weigh that against the amount of money a settlement might cost.

Obviously no one on Paula's legal team saw the big picture.

Risk management means that when your opponents have a nuclear bomb in their arsenal, you do everything and anything to defuse it.

Long before the decision was made to allow Ms. Dean to take part in a deposition, someone on her legal and claims consulting team should have assessed the risk of that happening.

Looking at the case strictly from a dollar standpoint, it would have saved Deen millions to get the case settled.

Since Ms. Jackson is asking for $1.2 million, I suspect she would have taken a somewhat smaller amount, like a million dollars.

Writing that check would have saved Paula from a million problems.

I'm not passing judgment on what she did or did not do. That is not my universe. The job of a risk manager is to see whether duking it out in court or quietly settling an allegation is the best business strategy.

Even if Deen goes on to win the lawsuit and pay nothing, she has already paid with everything.

The irony is that I missed most of the back and forth on the Deen lawsuit while I was at the annual convention for the Kentucky Bar Association. I attended a fascinating session on the use of mediation.

Mediation is a concept that barely existed 20 years ago and now is universally used in every type of litigation. It has been the ultimate game changer in the legal profession. Cases rarely go to trial unless all attempts at settlement are exhausted.

The panel contained stars in injury litigation like former Kentucky Chief Justice Joseph Lambert and Louisville lawyer Vanessa Canley, but also tax and business attorneys.

I've been involved in the mediation process for 25 years, but it was an eye opener to see how it is used for every type of dispute, including settlement with the Internal Revenue Service.

In *The Art of War*, Sun Tzu said, "he who knows when he can fight and when he cannot will be victorious."

Paula Deen's risk management crew would have been smart to take advice from a wise Chinese general from the fifth century.

They lost a battle they should have never fought.

Credit Card Company Claimed to Have Talked to My Dead Mother

(2009)

"Oh, my love, my darling
I've hungered for your touch
A long, lonely time
Time goes by so slowly
And time can do so much
Are you still mine?"
-The Righteous Brothers

My mother allegedly died on April 2, 2006. I say allegedly because a collector representing MBNA said he talked to her on June 21, 2006.

Until I saw a letter from Dale Lamb, I felt pretty certain my mother was dead.

I viewed her lifeless body at the hospital. A funeral director, who I have known since the second grade, gave me an urn that supposedly contained her ashes. I have a death certificate from the state of Kentucky.

Despite all of that, Lamb claims to have talked to her on June 21st.

Thanks to MBNA and their collector—the ironically named, True Logic Financial Corporation—Mom is now in a category with Elvis Presley, Kurt Cobain and Jim Morrison. She has been deemed alive despite tremendous evidence to the contrary.

Mom would love being associated with Elvis, but would not have been wild about being categorized with Kurt and Jim.

It seems almost comical now, but I was really angry. My mother died without warning, and I miss her. If MBNA's collector is able to talk to her, I wish he would give me her number.

The story of my mom and MBNA is an example of why credit card companies need more regulation.

I was named administrator of Mom's estate after she supposedly died. I then received a letter saying MBNA had obtained an arbitration award against Mom.

No one in my family knew anything about a debt to MBNA. Mom was supposedly dead, so we could not ask her.

I hired a lawyer to contact MBNA and to give us some verification of the alleged debt and arbitration award. Two months went by with no response. The attorney followed up again, but MBNA never got back to us.

Instead of responding to my attorney, MBNA shifted the alleged debt to True Logic.

Taking MBNA and True Logic at their word, I'm curious as to what Mom said to Mr. Lamb. I hope they have a tape recording. Mom was known to use salty language, and I'm sure Mr. Lamb would have heard some.

I'm not as prone to foul language, but if MBNA ever calls me, I am going to make an exception.

After True Logic sent the letter for MBNA, I once again hired an attorney, and once again he sent a letter denying the alleged debt.

If MBNA wants to sue, I am not sure if they will go after the estate or have Mom declared "un-dead" since they are having conversations with her. I'm not sure how to proceed if Mom orally agreed to a payment plan. A judge will have to figure all that out.

The whole incident has made me wonder how often MBNA ignores the legal right of creditors to verify a debt. They have one collector send a letter, ignore the response, and then have another collector try again.

I suspect that collectors can sometimes convince an unsuspecting family or estate to pay money.

The first letter from MBNA sounded serious. It was enough for me to hire a lawyer. The only follow up I received from MBNA was the letter from Mr. Lamb saying he spoke to a woman who is legally dead.

On the other hand, it could be that Lamb did talk to mom. One of her favorite movies was *Ghost*. Mom may not be able to communicate with me, but Lamb might be a real-life version of the psychic that Whoopi Goldberg portrayed in the movie. By talking to Lamb, Mom may be sending a signal that she wants MBNA to put up or shut up.

Mom is one you never wanted to mess with; allegedly dead or allegedly alive.

Gatewood: The Last Free Man in America
(2012)

I'm mourning the loss, at age 64, of my friend, author and frequent Kentucky political candidate Gatewood Galbraith.

Anyone who wants to be a best-selling author needed to spend time around Gatewood. He had knack for understanding his audience that few others had.

My first book fair event ever was the 2006 Kentucky Book Fair. When I walked into the arena, I found they had me sharing a table with Gatewood, who was promoting his excellent autobiography, *The Last Free Man in America.*

I was horrified that I was perched next to a perennial gubernatorial candidate who advocated the legalization of marijuana and known to take a toke or two on his own.

Being with him turned out to be the best thing that ever happened in my book career.

The day launched an unusual friendship.

I had poked fun at Galbraith in the book I was selling, *The Unbridled World of Ernie Fletcher.* I confessed my sin to Gatewood who laughed and said, "Donnie, it's not the first time someone has poked fun at me."

Being perched next to Gatewood for eight hours was like getting a PhD in book marketing.

Gatewood took me under his wing. He had been to hundreds of book events passed along his wisdom.

Wisdom that I never forgot.

He talked with me about how to dress. He said to always wear

Rockport's shoes with hard soles and heavy socks. It made it easier to stand in place all day. If you see me at a book event, you will note that I follow Gatewood's advice to this day. Rather than sitting behind the table, Gatewood convinced me that I needed to stand on my feet the entire time, be outgoing and friendly, and look every potential customer in the eye.

He suggested wearing a big hat, like he did, to draw attention. I don't like hats, but decided that a conservative business suit was more up my alley and would draw attention in a crowded book fair.

Whatever we were doing worked. At the end of the day, we were two of the biggest selling authors at the book fair. He sold more than me, but I think he sold more than anyone.

The next year, 2007, when my *Son of a Son of a Gambler* book came out, Gatewood, Kentucky State Treasurer (and current *Huffington Post* contributor) Jonathan Miller and I teamed up for a three person, statewide Kentucky book tour.

We traveled from Prestonsburg to Paducah and signed books at numerous political rallies.

We had fun and it was fascinating to be with Gatewood on a daily basis. He also connected with people from every part of society. Working people were his natural base, but he could hang with the high and mighty. Everyone loved him.

Everyone knew him, too. I owned a political consulting company in the early 1990s and we did polling for local and statewide candidates. Gatewood was running for something and had 100 percent name recognition in Lexington, Kentucky. George Bush, the president, had 99 percent and the sitting Governor, Wallace Wilkinson, was at 98 percent.

The key to his personality was that he never took himself too seriously. Issues were serious, but Gatewood was not.

That's not to say he wasn't practical. I was in the car behind him at a broken stop light in Somerset. I sat for 20 minutes, waiting for him to make his turn. Finally, I drove around him and he followed me into a parking lot.

I yelled over, "the last free man in America would have run that red light." Gatewood responded, "The last free man in America did not want to give the police a chance to search the back of my car."

Galbreath was ignored or laughed off by better funded candidates and usually by the mainstream media.

Being with him on a regular basis, I realized how many great ideas he had. Gatewood had a strong populist message that blown off by those who stereotyped him, "the pro pot candidate."

He had many views held by both Occupy Wall Street and the Tea Party, long before either movement came along. His brand of populism might have caught on if he had been a slicker, better funded, campaigner. He chose to remain true to himself and his core values.

Gatewood ran his last campaign in 2011, as an independent, running for Kentucky's Governor. He got about nine percent of the vote. His views on issues like outlawing Mountaintop Coal Removal differed from the Republican and Democratic standard bearers and kept the issue in the forefront of the media.

He impacted the political agenda, even when that wasn't his intent.

I was recently putting together a list of people to invite to my wedding and Gatewood was on my A list. When my fiancé' asked about him, I said, "You can't have a party unless Gatewood's there."

I'm sure Gatewood has a party rocking in heaven right now. I hope that his legacy of pushing ideas and issues deemed "too controversial" will live on.

History will prove that he was a man ahead of his time. And a great guy to spend time with.

It's hard to ask for a better life than that.

Section Four

SOMEWHERE THERES SOMEBODY WHOS NOT TREATING SOMEBODY RIGHT

Legalized Loan Sharks and Payday Lending
(2011)

"He drinks beer and eats beanies
Chases it down with ol' Thunderbird wine
Carries brass knuckles and a .44 Runs
A loan shark business and a Mary Jane store"
-Charlie Daniels Band

The town where I grew up in Northern Kentucky was a haven for organized crime. My father was a bookie and professional gambler who worked in several of the area's "hot spots."

In a town full of hustlers, prostitutes and gamblers, the profession they looked down on was loan sharking.

It wasn't unusual for a loan shark to wind up floating in the Ohio River. One of the biggest names in the business, Frank "Screw" Andrews, a central character in journalist Hank Messick's non-fiction book, *Syndicate Wife*, "accidentally fell" out of a fourth-floor window.

If Andrews were in business today, he would be a captain of industry. Loan sharking is now legalized, in the form of "payday lenders."

The stock of payday lenders is traded on the New York Stock Exchange and NASDAQ. Many payday lending companies do business with Wall Street's biggest banks.

As Gary Rivlin notes in his outstanding book, *Broke USA*, "The working poor have become big business."

You wouldn't think that poor people would be a growth market, but businesses make big money off people who live paycheck to paycheck.

There is a whole segment of society that does not use traditional banking services. They cash their paychecks at Wal-Marts, liquor stores and payday lenders.

Andrews met his fate out of a hospital window in 1973. I'm sure when he fell out of that window he never dreamed that nearly 40 years later his business would operate legally in almost every city in the country.

Andrews knew how to bribe local officials with cash payments. He didn't live to see such bribery legalized in the form of lobbying and political fundraising.

Broke USA makes it clear that the public and those in the media don't care for payday lenders, much the way the prostitutes and hustlers hadn't.

The poverty industry has given huge contributions to lawmakers. According to the Citizens for Responsibility and Ethics in Washington, payday lenders donated more than $1.5 million to federal office holders during the 2010 election cycle. Substantial donations were made to state and local lawmakers as well.

Until I read *Broke USA*, I didn't realize what a big hand the "too big to fail" banks have in creating the poverty industry. Many payday lenders would not exist if Wall Street had not given them the money to get started.

Citigroup, JP Morgan Chase and Bank of America are just some of the big banks that make huge profits, directly or indirectly, from the poverty industry.

The banks that fund the poverty industry have another common bond. They received bailout money from the American taxpayers in 2008.

If there was ever a shining example of why you should move your money from Wall Street, legalized loan sharking is a good one.

The people peddling poverty products have figured out there is a strain of Americans who are the financial equivalent of drug addicts. They will pay any price, fee, or interest rate as long as they can get an immediate fix. They don't care about tomorrow. They just want money today.

Another insight I got from *Broke USA* is that many people use payday lenders because they don't have access to traditional banks. I didn't realize that many banks won't give a checking account to people with bad credit.

Since the alleged "financial reform" that passed Congress in 2010, banking services for lower income people are getting worse.

"Too big to fail" banks are charging fees for checking, raising the minimum balance required to get free checking and hitting consumers with a bunch of nickel and dime charges.

Those nickels and dimes will add up to billions in profits for the banks we bailed out in 2008.

In reaction to financial reform, the head of JP Morgan Chase, Jamie Dimon, seemed to speak for all of Wall Street when he told the *New York Times*, "If you're a restaurant and you can't charge for the soda, you're going to charge more for the burger."

The burger is going to come out of the hides of the banks' poorest customers.

As payday lenders and others in the poverty business have found, it is easy to stick it to poor people. They have the fewest options.

More and more of them will fall out of the traditional banking system altogether.

"Financial reform" is a boon for people in the payday loan business. When people fall out of the world of traditional banking, they are still going to need bank-like services. Payday lenders will be in position to fill the gap.

Gary Rivlin and I have become friends since I did a review of *Broke USA* for Huffington Post. We both agree that payday lending is not going to go away unless the government steps up to the plate to regulate it.

In 2006, the U.S. Department of Defense realized that soldiers had a problem with payday lenders. They found that 17 percent of all military personnel were using payday loans, and soldiers' financial stresses were impacting their ability to function while fighting in Iraq and Afghanistan.

It was estimated that payday lenders were charging members of the U.S. military interest rates between 360 percent and 720 percent. Congress cut it down to a maximum of 36 percent.

Despite losing the military market, payday lenders showed they still had plenty of clout. It would have been simple for Congress to extend that 36 percent cap to all Americans, but Congress did not.

Instead, the battle has become one each state must fight individually.

I suspect if you let everyone vote on the issue, payday lenders would go away quickly.

Broke USA detailed an Ohio referendum capping payday lenders at 28 percent. The referendum got 63 percent of the vote. The study of how Ohio did it is a roadmap for other states trying to do the same thing.

Unfortunately for the people fighting payday lending, most states don't offer ballot initiatives and referendums. They elect legislators and ask them to represent us.

Many of the groups fighting payday lending are part of larger coalitions with a litany of other legislative interests. Fighting payday lending is merely one of many issues on their plates.

The payday lenders are all-in. It's life or death for them. They hire the best lobbyists.

Payday lenders have a well-organized, well-financed front, and they are going to fight with everything they've got. They make lots of contributions to all the right people.

One of the reasons it was easy for Congress to put a 36 percent cap on payday lending for military people is that it was easy to imagine a soldier serving in Iraq or Afghanistan being taken advantage of.

If you are dealing with a payday lender, the idea that you might achieve wealth, with or without Wall Street, is very remote. It is hard to get ahead when you are paying 300 percent or more in fees and interest payments.

Wealth cannot be sustained over a long period of time when the poorest of a community are exploited.

I've yet to see an election lost on the payday lending issue. That needs to happen before elected officials will take the opponents seriously.

The OxyContin Letters
(2007)

"When things go wrong, don't walk away
That will only make it harder"
-Robin Lane and the Chartbusters

I recently wrote about how the makers of OxyContin agreed to a wimpy $600 million settlement with the federal government. Purdue Pharma, the makers of OxyContin, was selling an addictive drug. The top executives knew it was addictive, and the company sold almost $10 billion of the stuff.

Their lawyer, presidential candidate Rudolph Giuliani, negotiated a plea that kept people at Purdue from going to jail.

Giuliani cut a deal that street pushers would drool over. The fine is a small percentage of their sales, and the drug is still on the market.

In the language of the street pusher, the people at Purdue copped a plea, paid a fine and went back on the street.

In the wake of the OxyContin executives' admission to committing a crime, Congressmen Hal Rogers of Kentucky and Frank Wolff of Virginia made a reasonable request.

They want OxyContin to be prescribed only for severe pain, not moderate pain as it is now.

Rogers said that one of the advantages of the change would be that it would cut the number of drugs being diverted to the black market.

Rogers and Wolff asked the Food and Drug Administration (FDA) to look into the matter.

Amazingly, Purdue Pharma, the makers of OxyContin, the same company that just let Giuliani cop a plea on their behalf, are fighting Rogers and Wolff.

Instead of thanking God for Rudy's great connections and the laptop tendencies of the prosecution, the people at Purdue want the FDA to ignore the congressmen.

Here is something I can't ignore. After I wrote my column, I started hearing from people all over the world.

A reader in Texas wrote the following:

> My sister was very much addicted to Oxycontin that she was obtaining legally from her doctor. She was living with my 72-year-old mother as she was unable to hold a job. Her boyfriend was also addicted to various drugs. One night she refused to give him more of her Oxycontin, and he left to later return and cut the throats of my mother and sister.

The OxyContin problem is not confined to the United States. A reader in Canada wrote:

> My son was addicted to Oxycontin for about three years. He is 22 months clean now, but only because he is on the methadone maintenance program. We live in a small town and have to travel two hours each way weekly for him to be urine tested and to see the doctor. He was hooked so hardcore, it is amazing he is still alive. He is clean right now, but he is a totally different person, often filled with anger. In our town of 6,500 people, the drug of choice among our kids is Oxycontin!

Not everyone liked my column. A financial consultant in New York City called me a jerk, but didn't specify why. Either he likes OxyContin or likes Giuliani. Maybe both.

An Arizona reader told me his doctor had prescribed OxyContin for his back pain, but that he was careful to explain that the drug could be addictive. Thus, the man used OxyContin without incident.

After reading horror story after horror story, I can't imagine a scenario where I would willingly take OxyContin. I can understand doing so if you and your doctor weigh the risks and the benefits.

For moderate pain there has to be a better solution than OxyContin. Even if the government just limited the supply, it would be a big step forward.

It takes a lot of gall to keep fighting after your company and its top executives have agreed to a $634.5 million fine—not to mention the fact that everyone who was charged was well-connected enough to avoid serving jail time.

Purdue apparently has that kind of gall.

The people at Purdue admitted to willfully doing something that harmed people. They ought to do more than pay a fine; they ought to show leadership and clean up some of the mess they started.

Instead, they want the FDA's blessing to keep on selling OxyContin to people with moderate pain.

The people at Purdue need to realize that when things go wrong, you don't walk away.

That will only make it harder.

Sticking It to Poor People
(2004)

"So welcome back baby
To the poor side of town"
-Johnny Rivers

Technology has made it easier for some businesses to take advantage of the poor. This is especially true with bank credit cards.

I know someone who has a credit card with a $650 credit limit with Orchard Credit Cards, which is owned by Household Finance, which is owned by Household International, which is owned by HSBC Holdings, a huge company based in England.

This is his only credit card and he has been paying the minimum payment each month. He has not been late with a payment in over a year.

His credit card statement showed the annual interest rate on the card is 18.90 percent. This means the bank is making about 16 percent in interest over what they pay for money deposited in their bank. That is a very high rate, but Household makes it worse by accessing a number of fees.

He ran the card to the limit last Christmas, but has been trying to pay it down since then. After several months, he got his debt down to about $600. In May, Household charged him an $89 annual "membership" fee to renew his card.

$89 equals 14 percent of his credit line just to have the credit card available to him. To make matters worse, Household slapped on a $28.70 fee on him (about four percent of his credit line) as the $89 fee caused him to go over the $650 limit.

Even though he has been a good customer, Household wants to take advantage of him by charging 18 percent of his total credit line just to keep the card open. They did not increase his credit limit so he can't use the card to buy things. Household targeted this card to people trying to improve their credit history, but now his credit report is damaged because the excessive fee put him over his credit limit.

The fee is too small to get an attorney to help him fight it. He tried writing Household, but they have outsourced customer service to people who don't respond to letters. He called and talked to a woman who said she would waive his fees if he cancelled his card which would leave him with no credit card. When he asked to speak to someone about waiving the fees and keeping the card, she said she was transferring him to another department and then hung up on him.

If he gets mad refuses to make his credit card payments, it completely destroys the credit history that he is trying to rebuild.

One of my favorite books is Joseph Nocera's 1994 book *A Piece of the Action*. Nocera touched on many subjects, including banks that used computers to target credit card customers. They were looking for hardworking people who make their payments on time but keep high balances on their credit cards.

Now that technology is better, it is easier for computers to pinpoint people who fit the bank's model. Technology has also made it possible for bill collectors to get more aggressive in their collection practices when people are late on payments.

I hear horror stories of collectors calling long lost family members and neighbors and using those people to put pressure on debtors. It is illegal, but the agencies that regulate banks aren't doing much to help poor people and the collectors know it. Even when regulators want to help, most poor people don't know the law or who to call.

In looking at their recent financial statements, it seems that Household International has been involved in litigation regarding consumer lending. I am not sure how this has turned out, but you would think that a company who has been recently sued would be smart enough not to charge 18 percent as annual fee.

The card holder is paying at least 18 percent in fees and then 18.90 percent in interest on top of that. With the balance increasing at that rate, the debt will never go away and he will never get a good credit history.

Companies like Household International will make sure that he never gets away from the poor side of town.

Section Five

Hurt
(2006)

"I hurt myself today
To see if I still feel
I focus on the pain
The only thing that's real"
-Trent Reznor

I had never listened to Reznor's band Nine Inch Nails until Johnny Cash did a cover of Reznor's song "Hurt." Reznor makes you understand the desperation of a drug addict.

You realize that the addict's entire life revolves around drugs and pain.

A few weeks ago, one of my clients died of a possible overdose on painkillers. She was under 30 years old and was hurt in an accident where she had just received a settlement. Her lawyers worked hard to make sure she was taken care of for the rest of her life. Her life only lasted only a month after her settlement.

I had only spent a few hours with her, but feel a sense of loss. I had met her family and can't imagine the pain they are in.

I also feel sorry for her lawyers. The case took years to settle, and they grew close to her while the battle went on. They worked hard to get a good settlement and even harder to make sure that she would be set up for life.

Many lawyers go the extra mile for their clients like these did. Although their effort was extraordinary, I often see good lawyers make that effort.

I get angry when people stereotype injury lawyers as "ambulance chasers" who are only out for themselves. Just like any kind of prejudice or slur, it is based on half-baked information and observation of a few bad apples. Just like in any occupation, there are good people and bad.

I know there are lawyers who would have sold out her case cheaply. She was not well-educated and would not have really known what her case was worth. They are others who would have settled the case but not really cared what she did with her money. It took a lot of extra time and effort to set up a trust on her behalf, and the lawyers did not get any money to do so. They did it because they wanted her to have a long and happy life.

That is why it hurts them to see her die so young.

I understand how she became dependant on painkillers. Her accident caused her to be in terrible pain, and she needed medicines to get through the day. It was a struggle for her to walk, and she needed someone to help her go to the bathroom.

Everyone is certain that she did not kill herself on purpose. Even with her injuries, she was upbeat, positive and had her life in order. Painkillers are hard to regulate, and I suspect she just took too much.

I see a lot of injured people get hooked on pain medicine trying to overcome an injury. Their lives then revolve around that addiction and they start to look for any means, legal or illegal, to get their hands on those drugs.

It is common for people to get addicted and die. If you glance through the obituaries and see how many dead are young people who are not terminally ill, it shows the magnitude of the how big the problem could be.

If anyone has a way to avoid a tragedy like my client, I am open to hearing about it. She was in pain and medicines were available to make her feel better. It is hard to blame her doctors for giving them to her. She was not taking illegal drugs so locking up pushers or passing more laws is not an answer. Her family loved her and her lawyers cared for her too. She had coped with many bad breaks but got a bad break that killed her.

I keep reading about government cutbacks in programs to treat addicts. I'm sure those programs are an easy target for cuts. Treatment can be expensive and many addicts will fall off the wagon. There is not a simple or easy answer.

There may not be an answer at all but I think we have to keep trying to find one. When someone is taken too soon, it is not just a loss for the individual; it is a loss for all of us.

We all feel the hurt.

Sunday Morning Coming Down
(2007)

"Well I woke up Sunday morning
With no way to hold my head that didn't hurt
And the beer I had for breakfast wasn't bad
So I had one more for desert"
-Kris Kristofferson (Johnny Cash)

On New Year's Day, there were many people with Sunday morning hangovers. For some people, it happens once a year. For others, it is an everyday experience.

Many people use booze or drugs when life is out of control. It is easier to pop a pill or have a beer than to tackle underlying problems.

New Year's Day is a time when people will make life changes. Diet classes and workout centers fill every January and people make resolutions to improve themselves.

My demon is my weight. Getting to obese would be an improvement.

Last January, I started a group called Don's Fat Guys Club. I wrote a column inviting men meet me and to share ideas about losing weight. Four men showed and the group was started.

This January, I am 22 pounds lighter and the group is going strong. We've added a few members (and looking for more), but every person in the group has lost weight.

If I can ever get below obese, they'll probably have me on *Oprah*. The Fat Guys have been an amazing success story.

Like most successful self-help groups, we do not charge a fee and give each other support.

We are different from 12-step groups in that we are competitive.

We put a dollar each in a pot. The person with the biggest weight loss that week gets the cash. It is a motivator. I won three weeks in a row and everyone was gunning for me on the fourth.

Motivation is the key to battling demons. I don't know what makes a person decide to get help, but it has to come from within. Once they decide, they need the support of others and from a higher power.

People who turn to booze, drugs and other poisons use them as a substitute for something missing in their lives.

Employees with substance abuse problems are a real dilemma. I've had good employees suddenly become bad employees when faced with a trauma in their personal lives. They started drinking or taking medications.

It was not just Sunday morning coming down, it is Monday, Tuesday and every other day as well. They were constantly hung over.

They did not come to work drunk or stoned, but not at the top of their game. Although we cared for them as people, the organization can't carry someone who is not pulling their weight.

It is not easy to suggest that someone start dealing with their problems. Most people with problems know they have problems. They don't appreciate your pointing it out to them.

You don't need to tell me I'm fat. My scale, clothes and broken chair will do that for me.

On the other hand, if you are a true friend or loved one, you want to do something to get the person to confront their issues.

Concern needs to be communicated in an effective manner.

I once suggested via email that a friend needed to find a therapist. Good intentions with bad implementation.

If I had gotten the email instead of sending it, I would have responded by sending the lyrics to the Aaron Tippin song "Kiss This."

My friend had a milder temperament.

A struggling person needs support from other people. That is one of the reasons that groups like Alcoholics Anonymous have had such tremendous success. They give a person with problems love and understanding.

The Fat Guys have worked because we root for each other, but have a competitive nature.

The result of a recent wager is that I am starting 2006 with a personal trainer. That ought to help my weight loss and overall fitness.

I hope people fighting drug and alcohol problems will use the New Year as an opportunity to look at their lives and battle their demons.

This could be the last year when they face another Sunday morning coming down.

Empathy for Society's Child
(2009)

"One of these days I'm gonna stop my listening
Gonna raise my head up high
One of these days I'm gonna raise up my glistening wings and fly
But that day will have to wait for a while
Baby I'm only society's child"
-Janis Ian

Janis Ian's songwriting broke ground in two crucial areas. "Society's Child" was about interracial dating in the 1960s. Her 1975 hit "At Seventeen" reflected on the angst of unpopular high school kids.

Both songs are relevant to a celebration I attended.

My longtime friend, Bob Babbage, was recently inducted into Lexington, Kentucky's Henry Clay High School Hall of Fame.

Bob had been elected to two of Kentucky's highest offices and is now the state's most successful lobbyist.

Like many adults who receive hall of fame awards, Bob was a geek in high school. He wasn't in the in-crowd and wasn't particularly cool. He was elected student council president and found his niche in politics.

Bob graduated in 1969, the year his all-white school merged with an all-black school. Bob talked about how that year influenced his decision to fight discrimination during his adult life.

The school honored another self-professed nerd, Billy Reed, class of 1961. One of Kentucky's most famous sportswriters, Billy had a long career writing for *Sports Illustrated* and several other publications.

Billy never played sports. He started covering them for the *Lexington Herald* in high school and still hasn't stopped.

There were only three African-American students in Billy's high school class. Before his induction, Billy attempted to track down all three to invite them to the dinner. One of the classmates had died, and one had no desire to relive painful childhood memories.

The third was Nanine Neal Watson. She came to the dinner all the way from Oakland, California. She brought with her to the dinner several family members, including her nephew, former Pittsburgh Steeler All-Pro, Dermontti Dawson.

Ms. Watson talked about how high school was unpleasant and how she appreciated the effort that Reed made to reach out to her, 48 years later.

Ralph Keyes' book, *Is There Life After High School?*, is based on the premise that high school is the four most important years in shaping a person's life.

If you look at Reed and Babbage, that holds true. Each chose professions (sports writing and politics) spawned from his high school experiences. They both came away from high school understanding what it was like to be an underdog.

If Billy had been a high school sports star, instead of someone who wrote about sports, I wonder if he would have noticed or felt the pain of his three classmates. I doubt it.

Being excluded is one of those things you never get out of your system. For many of us, it gave us compassion for those who got the same treatment.

I played sports, but was never a "cool kid" at any point in my life. As I grew up, I became an ardent adversary of discrimination. I am against any kind of discrimination, against any classifying of people, for any reason. It is a passion fueled by childhood experience.

Somewhere along the way, I took comfort in the idea that "the geeks would inherit the earth."

If you study the life of famous and successful people, very few were popular in high school. Of our recent presidents, I can only think of the elder George Bush as a potentially "cool" high school kid.

Although Barack Obama is the ultimate in adult cool, he notes in his book, *Dreams of My Father,* that it was not that way growing up. The product a biracial, single parent family, growing in the 1960s, Obama was the ultimate "Society's Child."

Thus, it wasn't a big surprise when Obama listed "empathy" as a qualification for his first pick to the Supreme Court.

Some right-wing pundits poke fun at the idea of "empathy" being a qualification. They suggest that Obama wants a justice who is wimpy and soft.

Obama is looking for is the same characteristic that Billy Reed and Bob Babbage showed at the banquet: The ability to feel what it is like to be on the outside.

I want someone on the United States Supreme Court who can look back at actions that were wrong, feel a sense of injustice and make amends, even if the act happened 40 or 50 years ago.

Time doesn't heal wounds. People do.

Empathy has been part of world culture for centuries.

Many major religions require confession of sins or have days of atonement. Twelve-step programs require addicts to make amends to people they wronged.

It's a good process for the person apologizing and a good process for the person accepting the apology.

Obama wants a Supreme Court Justice who can show the kind of empathy that some special people showed on a very special night.

For all of our sakes, I hope he finds one.

Playing the Hand God Dealt to You
(2009)

"Lord, I've seen fire
And I've seen rain"
-James Taylor

My father was a professional gambler. When faced with any kind of crisis, he would always say, "You have to play the hand that is dealt you."

A good philosophy. One that I have followed all my life.

In my career as a structured settlement and financial consultant, a number of my clients are brain injured or special needs children. I've been doing it since 1983. Many of the children I originally worked with are adults. I've watched the whole progression and they are generally doing well.

One of the fascinating things I have seen is that the parents, almost universally, step up to the plate and do what they need to do to make it better for their children.

Being the parent of a special needs child is one of the toughest jobs in the world. It is a lifelong assignment. You don't ship the child out the door at 18 or 30 or 50. Or ever.

The parents need to be involved until the day they die or their child dies.

I've dealt with hundreds of parents of special needs children. They take the hand that is dealt to them. And usually turn them into aces.

So much comes down to having a positive attitude. Any child, but especially a special needs child, forces parents to understand there is a world beyond themselves.

One of my Facebook friends is the parent of a severely injured child and she summed it up perfectly in a post on my Facebook page:

> "I think a lot about the phrase from expectant parents 'as long as the baby is healthy.' No one wants their child to suffer or experience a handicap, but the love and bond you feel with that child that was not born healthy, is like no other. It gives you a whole new meaning and depth to life that honestly I would not trade."

I think about the "playing the hand that is dealt to you" philosophy in terms of our economic crisis. From Wall Street to Washington to Main Street, people were being dealt decent hands but kept trading cards in a quest to hit blackjack.

We have a lot of people tapped out in a quest to chase the unrealistic.

People on Wall Street were receiving millions in bonuses. They were given more money than a person could spend in a lifetime but looked for more. People in Washington had lobbyists whispering in their ear that the laws of economics didn't apply. People on Main Street were buying expensive houses and racking up credit card debt.

None of them were playing the hand that was dealt to them.

The decisions made were motivated by individual greed. The people were not looking at world beyond themselves. They were blinded into believing that a big bonus or a fancy new car was important to some aspect of life.

They don't see the world that the parent of a special needs child sees it. Realism trumps materialism in that universe.

Having a special needs child could be a burden or a blessing. Parents with healthy children deal with issues like drugs, substance abuse, sexually transmitted diseases and children who grow up to be selfish, lazy and unmotivated. I see the parents with adult children living at home for no apparent reason. I see grandparents raising grandchildren when the parents are unwilling or unable.

I've seen a lot of people who thought they had a winning hand with healthy children, but wind up busting out.

To raise a special needs child requires a degree of unselfishness and level headedness that the average person doesn't have.

I would have loved for the parent of a special needs child to have been handling our economy for the past few years. Even without special training, they have the right attitude to make good decisions.

If nothing else, they couldn't do worse than the gang on Wall Street and in Washington.

Parents of a special child understand that you play the hand that God dealt to you.

We need to get that message to the people on Wall Street, Washington and Main Street.

Addicted to Spending
(2009)

"They tried to make me go to rehab
I said no, no, no"
-Amy Winehouse

I don't know if they have rehab for spending addicts. If not, someone ought to start one.

I was flipping though the news channels when I heard a guest demand that we give tax rebates to poor people.

"Rich people accumulate wealth. Poor people accumulate things," he said.

He had a trickle up theory of economics. His believed that poor people will go a wild spending spree. The money will burn a hole in a poor person's pocket while wealthy people would sock it away.

Most poor people need their income just to survive, but there are many who are broke because they don't handle money well.

There is a financial dividing line that separates savers and spenders.

The savers wind up with wealth and the spenders wind up with debt.

The line between affluence and broke is getting bigger. If a poor people want to go a go on a spending spree, there are plenty of credit card companies, payday lenders, "buy here, pay here" car lots and subprime lenders to help them along.

The economy is in recession because some avenues of credit are drying up. Too many people got in over their heads and can't make payments. Companies like Citigroup bet that the fun would never stop. The bet cost their shareholders billions.

Giving rebate checks to the poor won't bail Citigroup out.

If I get a rebate check, I'll send it back to the government. They will eventually want it back to someday pay for the giveaway.

People on their way to wealth have good savings habits. People living beyond their means blow money on stuff they don't need.

Spending is instant gratification, like snorting cocaine. One shopper told me that she got a high from shopping like a high from drugs.

Shopping doesn't work for me. When I walk into a store, the hatred of shopping contorts my face to resemble a mass murderer or a professional wrestler. People run out of the aisles when they see me. I buy what I came to find and get out as quick as possible.

My goal is to accumulate wealth, not things.

When I was growing up, I used to think some people didn't have good jobs. They lived in run down houses and often had their cars repossessed I found out that they made as much money as my parents. The people who lived in run down houses spent money on gadgets they didn't use and motorboats that never made it in the water.

They lent money to "family and friends" even though they should have paying their own bills first. They had no sense of long-term planning and ultimately had no money.

Spending beyond your means is an addiction. A spending addiction is probably as hard to cure as a drug addiction. It requires changing your lifestyle.

Money is a leading cause of divorce. The stress of debt pushes people to escape reality with booze or drugs.

When the economy slows downs, the addiction becomes a crisis. People who were keeping the balls in the air suddenly can't. They have no backup systems.

I've frequently hired a casual laborer. He is good at his craft and for 20 years made really good money. None of which he saved. Whenever I saw him, he talked about skiing trips, his bass boat or his brand new trucks.

Now the economy has turned. His house is being foreclosed on and they repossessed his trucks. He has no savings or credit.

His focus was on accumulating possessions. Now he doesn't have those possessions. Or any money either.

The nation's economic system has also gotten addicted to shopping.

America's ebb and flow depends on citizens who accumulate things. If those people stopped buying and running up their credit card at the same time, the banks and stock markets would collapse.

That won't happen soon. Shopping addiction is not going away.

There is going to be a day when it all hits the fan. Americans are competing against workers in countries like China who have great savings habits.

To turn the economy around, Americans need to find a spender's version of rehab.

Rudolph Giuliani and the OxyContin People
(2007)

"Well, now if I were the President of this land
You know, I'd declare total war on the pusher man
God damn the pusher"
-Steppenwolf

Rudolph Giuliani wants to be President of the United States. He claims to be tough on criminals.

In some cases, he is—unless the criminals hire him to be their lawyer.

The people who make OxyContin did something horrible: they sold a drug they knew was addictive and acted like it wasn't.

I thought the makers of OxyContin got off easy when they agreed to a $600 million fine. Three of their top executives paid an additional $34 million. No jail time.

It was a wimpy settlement with a company that sold over $9 billion dollars of OxyContin.

The reason for the government's light tough was found in the *Washington Post*. Rudolph Giuliani was a lawyer for the company that makes OxyContin.

The *Post* said that Giuliani personally met with government lawyers more than half a dozen times.

The story gets more outrageous if you read the "The Blotter" blog by Brian Ross of ABC News. Ross said that Giuliani and his team have advised OxyContin's makers for the past five years.

According to Ross, Giuliani personally met with the head of the federal Drug Enforcement Administration (DEA) when the DEA's drug diversion office began a criminal investigation into the company.

No wonder the OxyContin people got a sweetheart deal: Giuliani is not a guy government bureaucrats want to mess with.

Imagine yourself as a government official and Rudolph Giuliani walks in to negotiate with you. There is a very good chance Giuliani could be soon be President of the United States.

That means you are sitting across the table from a guy who might be your boss.

If a frontrunner for President of the United States wants a good deal, you are going to think hard before you say no.

The OxyContin makers may not have strong morals, but they do have brains. They hired one of the best lawyers money could buy.

The irony is that the old Rudolph Giuliani would have loved to have gone after the OxyContin makers. Rudy got his start as a federal prosecutor and liked to go after white-collar types.

Here was the perfect situation for the old Rudy. You had a company that knew their drug would make people addicts. The company officers devised a plan to market OxyContin to as many people as possible.

The old Rudy would have shut down the company and thrown all the officers in jail.

The new Rudy cut his clients a sweet deal: no one will spend a day in jail. The federal government considered the crime to be a misdemeanor like noodling. Prosecutors are beating their chest about a $600 million fine that is only about six percent of OxyContin total sales.

$600 million is just a cost of doing business. It won't even hurt the company's stock price.

$130 million was set aside for the claims of victims. That sounds incredibly low. Everyone who went to the doctor for a bad back and came out a drug addict has a claim. There are thousands of people addicted to OxyContin, and hundreds died.

When you see round ups of street dealers, many are addicts trying to feed their addiction. Many of those addictions wouldn't have happened if Giuliani's clients had not been greedy, reckless and stupid.

A better punishment would be to make the company execs take their own product for a couple months and then kick the habit in a county jail cell.

It would give them an idea of what really happened.

The Steppenwolf song "The Pusher" is a graphic depiction of someone addicted. The character wants the President of the United States to declare war on pushers. That doesn't just mean rounding up junkies and street dealers: it means doing something about big pharmaceutical companies, too.

Giuliani is not the President to make that happen.

When the OxyContin people go to meet their maker, I hope that the response they get is, "God damn the pusher." It would make up for the government letting them off the hook.

Al Smith and Don on *Comment on Kentucky*

Bob Edwards and Don at Kentucky Book Fair

Don and Ed McClanahan

Don and Joe Elliott in WHAS studio

Don and Karen McNay with Mr. Tony Bennett

Don speaking at Joseph Beth

Don's first Kentucky Book Fair in 2006, with Gatewood Galbraith, a man who became Don's friend and mentor

In Las Vegas, taping a segment on lottery winners for RAI -Italy television

In studio on *CBS Morning News*, New York

Kentucky Journalism Hall of Fame Luncheon with Ferrell Wellman, Byron Crawford and Samantha Swindler

Madison County Attorney Marc Robbins & *Life Lessons from the Golf Course* **coauthor Clay Hamrick**

Pete Rose, Don and the Music Professor Jim LaBarbara

Some of Don's family at *Wealth Without Wall Street* kickoff in Kentucky

WYMT General Manager Neil Middleton and Don on *Issues and Answers*, the Mountain Edition

Don and Arianna Huffington

At Lexington Rotary with good friends like Jim Host and Al Smith

Section Six

The Five Things to Do When You Win the Lottery
(2007)

The Powerball jackpot is climbing to record levels as I release a new book, *Life Lessons from the Lottery: Protecting your money in a Scary World.*

It is a follow up to my 2008, best-selling book called *Son of a Son of a Gambler: Winners, Losers and What to Do When You Win the Lottery.*

If you win the jackpot, follow this advice carefully.

1. Tell as few people as possible (preferably no one) that you won.
2. Take a deep breath and make some good, long-term decisions. You don't have to cash the ticket today.
3. Work with a financial adviser who works with more money than you have.
4. Take the money in annual payments instead of the lump sum.
5. Use some of the money to give back to society.

Those are five simple rules that about 90 percent of lottery winners don't follow.

1. Tell as few people as possible (preferably no one) that you won.
If you can keep your jackpot quiet, do so. As I told Rebecca Jarvis during *an interview on CBS Morning News*, "Once you have told the world that received money that you never expected to have, everyone has their hand out, and you are not prepared for it." I once told a young, single, publicly known lottery winner that he had just become the best-looking man in his city. He was realistic enough to know that that wasn't really the case.

2. Take a deep breath and make some good, long-term decisions. You don't have to cash the ticket today.

Some people can't wait to cash their ticket. There have been stories about people camping out in front of lottery offices overnight with the winning ticket. Most lotteries allow you several months or a year to cash a winning ticket. The money will still be there in a month or so. Take some time to figure out what you are going to do with the money and how you are going to do it.

3. Work with a financial advisor who works with more money than you have.
There are financial advisors, estate planning attorneys and trust officers who have worked with $100,000,000 or more. The scorekeeper for your local bowling league is not one of them. People will often hire a friend as opposed to someone who really knows about big money. A good friend would tell you the situation is too complicated for them and help you find some real experts. A lottery winner has tax, estate and planning issues that they didn't have the week before.

4. Take the money in annual payments instead of the lump sum.
Roughly 98 percent of all lottery winners ignore this advice, but I continue to preach the mantra. Taking the payments over time allows you to adjust, with the money coming in on a gradual basis. If you make mistakes and lose all your money the first few years, you have 24 more opportunities to get it right. There are also some tax advantages to taking the money over time, as you are taxed on the money as you receive it. That may not be relevant with $100 million, as you are always going to be in the highest tax bracket, but a person who gets $1 million and takes $50,000 a year might be able to save overall.

5. Give back to society.
There are many people who have accumulated great wealth, like Rockefeller and Carnegie in the 20th century and Bill Gates and Warren Buffett in this century, who are giving away most of their money during their lifetimes. People who use their wealth to make an impact on society are far happier than those who use it to show off to the neighbors.

Amanda Clayton: Death by Being a Lottery Winner

(2012)

"I can feel the hand, of a stranger
And it's tightening, around my throat
Heaven help me, Heaven help me"
-Grand Funk Railroad

Amanda Clayton was not your typical millionaire. In her short life, she won a million dollar lottery in Michigan, was convicted of collecting state welfare money AFTER she got the million dollars and embroiled in a plethora of drama and legal battles.

Now she is dead, at age 25, of a drug overdose.

I've devoted much of my life to studying why people run through large sums of money. Especially lottery winners. I've written two best-selling books, along with a new book, *Life Lessons from the Lottery*, which will be out on Kindle on November 10.

And they all focus on why people run through money needlessly.

I keep thinking that if Amanda had read one of them, she might be alive, but probably not. She lived a troubled life. Getting the lottery money added rocket fuel to her problems.

Like so many lottery losers, Amanda made the first big mistake when she won the lottery: She let the world know she won.

In her home state of Michigan, it's possible for state lottery winners to collect their winnings anonymously, expect for Mega Millions and Powerball winners.

Thus, Amanda would have been better off to quietly take her winnings, but it didn't work out that way.

If you go online, you can find a happy and attractive Amanda from

September of last year. She was smiling, holding a huge million dollar check from the Michigan Lottery.

Now she is in a coffin, holding a lily. For eternity. To me, the big check and lily are correlated.

Telling the world that you have money that you never expected to have is asking for trouble. Like Abraham Shakespeare, another lottery winner who wound up dead in Florida, people thinking that your money should be "our" money seem to come out of the woodwork.

From various news accounts, it seemed like Amanda had a ton of newfound "friends." All wanting to take advantage of her.

Although Amanda was not shy about making headlines with her check, there was one group of people she "forgot" to mention it to.

The food stamp and public assistance office.

According to the Detroit News, Clayton plead no contest to fraud in June after state prosecutors accused her of receiving $5500 in food and medical benefits after she won the lottery.

Millionaires are not supposed to collect food stamps. If Amanda had tried to rip off the government as a Wall Street banker, her crime would have been ignored and she probably would have received a government bailout.

She got nine months probation instead. She wound up not staying alive until the end of her sentence.

It's sad to see a 25-year-old throw their life away. I'm not sure that winning the lottery was the source of her problems, but I see it happen too many times.

People who win the lottery lose perspective on normal things in life. They start to think that rules don't apply to them. In Amanda's case, she thought she could outsmart the welfare people and do serious drugs without consequence.

She lost her bet both times.

It's been said that roughly 90 percent of people who win the lottery will run through it in five years or less. I tell lottery winners five things to protect themselves.

1. Don't tell anyone you won. If you can collect the money anonymously, do so.
2. Stop and think for a minute before rushing down to collect the check.
3. Don't take the lump sum payment. Take the money over time instead.
4. Find an advisor who has worked with more money than what you have. If you win $100 million, find an advisor who has clients with $150 million. They are out there.
5. Use your money to give something back to society.

It looks like Amanda went five for five in things that she did wrong.

Now she is no longer with us.

How to Pick a Kentucky Derby Winner
(2009)

"When you're sitting back
In your rose pink Cadillac
Making bets on Kentucky Derby Day"
-Rolling Stones

As the son of a son of a gambler, people ask me for betting advice.

Although I started going to race track before I was able to walk, I don't know that much about the horse industry. I go the track a few times a year and bet small amounts.

Most of my equine knowledge was gleamed when I worked on the cleanup crew at the Kentucky Horse Park. I can tell you what horses make the biggest mess.

Although there are people more qualified to give Derby tips, like political or financial commentators, I won't let lack of expertise stop me.

I came to the conclusion in the mid-1980s that I wanted to live my life in Kentucky, I needed to know how to bet on horses.

 I found a book called *Racetrack Betting: The Professors' Guide to Strategies* by Peter Asch and Richard E. Quandi.

It was written by two statistics professors and not the easiest book to read. I can sum up the advice in two statements.

1. Bet on the horse that everyone else is betting on.

2. Bet on the horse to show, not to win or place.

The book bases the ability to pick horses on a theory known as the wisdom of crowds.

The wisdom of crowds concept is really popular now. It is a driving force for web sites like Google.

The idea is that marketplace will move towards the best outcome.

If a horse moves from 10 to 1 to 2 to 1, it is probably a good horse to bet on.

Betting to show is a practice that I follow religiously.

The professors said that betting to show will produce a winner 52 percent of the time. That is better than any other kind of bet.

The professors hate jackpots like the Pick-6. Just like the lottery, big odds draw a lot of excitement and attention.

Just like the lottery, you don't see many people winning them.

The professors frown on exactas, daily doubles or any bet that exhibits large risk.

Like in the investment world, the winner at race track is the person with a conservative style and discipline.

When I go to the track, I don't look at the racing form, jockeys, past history or pick horses with funny names. (My mother was a sucker for horses with funny names.) I just follow the odds.

I usually win enough money to pay for lunch.

My father, a professional gambler, absolutely HATED my betting system. He and I would go to Keeneland every session and we never picked the same horse. He would bet $100 on a horse and lose. I would bet $10 and win.

It drove him absolutely crazy.

Dad liked the excitement of big odds and big payoffs. He knew everything about the horse's past performance, their breeding and who was riding them.

Dad was superstitious and started to believe that my system was jinxing him. If Dad ever met the professors, he would have punched them in the nose.

I stuck to my system. I stick to it today. Betting to show fits with my overall philosophy about investing. Slow and steady works in the financial markets and works at the track too.

For whatever reason, my system has failed me at Kentucky Derby's. The last one I remember winning was Sunday Silence in 1989. I didn't pick Sunday Silence because of my system. His owner, Arthur Hancock III, had graduated from Vanderbilt and I had received a Masters Degree from Vandy the year before.

I picked the horse because of an alumni connection to a man I had never met. It was a stupid reason for picking a horse, but produced one of my few winners.

Thus, on Derby Day, my advice is forget all the high-powered systems and give it your best guess.

Death by Lottery
(2010)

"Ooh, ooh that smell
Can't you smell that smell?
Ooh, ooh that smell
The smell of death surrounds you"
-Lynyrd Skynyrd

He even had a tragic name.

Abraham Shakespeare should have been on top of the world. In 2006, he won $16.9 million in the Florida lottery.

Last week, they found his body. Buried five foot deep and under concrete.

His death wasn't a big surprise. He had been missing since April, but no one bothered to report him missing until November 9.

Shakespeare had acquired a huge entourage, but they didn't really miss him. They just missed his money.

I hope Mr. Shakespeare is now in heaven. From the day he stood in front of a news conference, holding a big replica of a Florida lotto check, his life became a living hell.

Like every other lottery winner, Shakespeare said the money wouldn't change him.

Like every other lottery winner, it did.

Not for the better.

Right off the bat, one of Shakespeare's co workers's sued, claiming that Abraham had stolen the winning ticket from him. The jury ruled for Shakespeare six months later, but by then, according to the *New*

York Daily News, "there were people constantly asking for a piece of his fortune."

Dorice Donegan "Dee Dee" Moore was a person who apparently got a good chunk of it.

Moore is considered "a person of intense interest" concerning Shakespeare's disappearance and death. Troy McKay Young, a Lakeland, Florida police office was arrested for unlawful compensation, as he was alleged to sell confidential information, such as Shakespeare's license plate number, to Dee Dee Moore.

It seemed like everyone wanted a piece of Shakespeare.

According to published reports, Dee Dee Moore had a joint bank account with Shakespeare and acquired nearly $2 million of his money.

They found Shakespeare's body on land owned by her boyfriend.

I've written a book about what to do when you win the lottery. Shakespeare was a textbook example of doing everything backwards.

I tell lottery winners to keep it confidential. Shakespeare had a news conference and waved a big check.

I tell people to take the annual payments. Shakespeare took a lump sum.

I tell people to get professional advice. Moore, who seemed to be his advisor, apparently went to great lengths, and possibly used illegal methods, to track him down.

Professional advisors don't track down clients. Clients are referred to them by attorneys or other financial professionals.

I tell people to use their money to make a positive impact on society.

Shakespeare talked about setting up a foundation to help poor people, but it never happened.

Instead, the money was wasted and frittered away.

Just like his life was wasted and frittered away.

The day that Shakespeare cashed his winning ticket, the smell of death surrounded him.

Section Seven

Save Our Soldiers from Peter Lynch
(2004)

"Some folks inherit star spangled eyes
Ooh, they send you down to war, Lord
And when you ask them, how much should we give
Oh, they only answer, more, more, more"
-John Fogerty

We ask a lot of our armed service people. They ship out to foreign countries and some come back in body bags. The least we can do is assure that they don't get ripped off.

Diane Henriques wrote in *The New York Times* about salespeople peddling financial products to soldiers. It is a series that should be nominated for the Pulitzer Prize.

Part of the series focused on an obscure product called contractual mutual funds. These plans lock the soldiers into buying funds over 15 or 20 years. They pay a 50 percent first year commission to the people who sell them. It is almost impossible for those funds to do as well as other investments.

The Securities and Exchange Commission tried to abolish the plans back in 1966 and allow purchasers 45 days to get out of them. They are so obscure that the mutual fund industry quit tracking them in 1985 and most investment experts, like Vanguard founder John Bogle, say they would never recommend one.

The New York Times report focused more on the fund salespeople than it did on the billion dollar companies like Fidelity that manage the contractual funds. Fidelity's Destiny II fund was the biggest seller.

It is like writing about the war on drugs and focusing on street pushers instead of the drug lords. Big name sponsors like Fidelity make it easy for fund peddlers to sell the product.

I hope that *The New York Times* did not ignore companies like
Fidelity that buy ads from them to go after the no name salespeople
that do not. I am really surprised that Henriques, who wrote the best-
selling book *Fidelity World*, did not focus more of the series on
Fidelity and their Vice Chairman, Peter Lynch.

Lynch's investment success has been a major focus of Fidelity's
marketing. He hangs out with Hollywood types like Lily Tomlin in
Fidelity's commercials. He is the public face of Fidelity, just like
Martha Stewart is the public face of her company.

If Peter Lynch wants Fidelity to stop selling contractual funds, they
will stop. He is a smart guy who has to know the funds are a bad
deal. If Lynch thinks their contractual funds are such a great deal, he
ought to get Fidelity to switch all 200 of their funds to be managed
the same way. Don't hold your breath waiting for that to happen.

Fidelity touts how much money it gives to charity on its web site.
Before they take credit for that, they need to give a fair shake to our
armed services.

I cannot say that Peter Lynch told Fidelity to market the contractual
plans to soldiers. He may not know they are selling them. However,
he is Vice Chairman of the company and has worked there most of
his life. When he ran his Magellan fund, he was famous for knowing
every little detail about the 1400 companies in which he invested.
It's hard for me to believe he does not know what his own company
is doing.

Lynch may actually believe that the contractual funds are good
deals. It would go against everything he has ever said or done, but
maybe it is true.

There is a simple way for Lynch to convince us. The University of
Kentucky basketball team says that if a citizen can prove a ticket
holder is scalping tickets, the person who turns them in gets the
tickets of the scalper.

Lynch could offer a similar deal to the armed services. If Lynch can't prove the contractual funds are as good as Fidelity's other funds, some soldier gets to come home and Lynch gets shipped out to Iraq in their place.

I don't think Lynch will sign up for that deal. Lynch and Fidelity are wrong and need to fix the problem. If Lynch is the ethical man that his biographers say he is, he will get Fidelity to stop selling contractual funds.

It is our patriotic duty to encourage him.

Sending a Message to Peter Lynch
(2004)

"There's gonna be Hell
When you hear mother freedom start ringing her bell
It's gonna feel like the whole wide world is raining down on you
Brought to you courtesy of the Red, White and Blue"
-Toby Keith

My regular readers have to be surprised that a Toby Keith lyric would start off my column. Mr. Keith and I disagree on several topics, but Toby advanced his career taking up the cause of soldiers. He would not be happy to know that a billion dollar company is taking advantage of them.

Last week, I wrote about the Fidelity mutual funds selling a product called contractual mutual funds to armed services personnel. Fidelity has gotten away with it as the product is hard to understand, but I put a special section on my web site to help explain it. Most investment professionals would not allow their clients to put money in a product that pays 50 percent to the people selling it.

I took Peter Lynch, Fidelity's Vice-Chairman to task for allowing Fidelity to sell it to people who are putting their lives on the line for us.

Peter Lynch is a famous multimillionaire who hangs out with Hollywood stars. He does not care what some writer in Kentucky thinks about him. Fidelity is making big profits by selling the funds.

If we want to help our soldiers, it will take a group effort to get Lynch's attention.

Instead of Toby Keith, I almost used another country song, Randy Travis's "Points of Light." There is a line in that song that describes why I want you to help.

"If you see what's wrong

And you try to make it right
You will be a point of light"

I can't pull this off by myself. I need your help. I need a "thousand points of light," or at least one or two points of light, to get Lynch to notice us.

Lynch may do the right thing if enough people let him know we care. I have three different strategies to get his attention.

1. Write or call Peter Lynch directly Ask Peter to quit selling their Fidelity Destiny II fund, (their contractual fund) to soldiers. Peter doesn't give out his phone number or his email, but Fidelity has an office staffed with public relations flunkies. They can forward a message.

You can email (FidelityCorporateAffairs@fmr.com) or call (617) 563-5800. You can tell them to look at my web site (www.donmcnay.com) for more information.

2. Since Peter is not taking calls, a way to get his attention is to let people in Congress know about the problem. Fidelity is regulated at the federal and state levels and doesn't want those people mad at them.

Congressman Ben Chandler, a semi-regular reader of this column, showed he was not afraid to go after special interests when he was Kentucky's Attorney General. You can email him (ben.chandler@mail.house.gov) or call his Lexington office at 859-219-1366.

Senator Mitch McConnell, one of the most powerful Senators in Washington, has to be concerned about soldiers stationed at Fort Campbell and Fort Knox. He can call Peter Lynch on the carpet anytime he feels like it. Give him a call at his Lexington office (859) 224-8286 or send him an email (senator@mcconnell.senate.gov).

3. I'll bet you didn't know that Fidelity was one of Kentucky's

largest employers. It employs over 4000 people in Northern Kentucky and got some big tax breaks to be there. Since they got those breaks from the state of Kentucky, it might be a good idea to let our State Representative Harry Moberly and Governor Ernie Fletcher know how you feel. You might also suggest that Kentucky ban contractual mutual funds. There are a lot of soldiers in the state and at least it would help them.

If you contact anyone, send me an email (don@mcnay.com) and let me know. It is our duty as Americans to let Peter Lynch know that our armed services people deserve better. I want Lynch to get so many messages that he thinks that the whole wide world is raining down on him.

Tell him it is brought to him courtesy of the Red, White and Blue.

Peter Lynch and the Culture of Greed
(2008)

Fidelity Vice Chairman Peter Lynch recently settled a complaint against him filed by the Securities and Exchange Commission.

Lynch was fined for receiving free trips and tickets.

Since Lynch likes freebies, I am surprised that he did not respond to my longstanding offer.

A one way ticket to Iraq.

I've written numerous columns bashing Lynch. His company peddled high commissioned mutual funds to soldiers during a time of war.

Fidelity sold contractual mutual funds. They had huge upfront loads. The funds were so bad that Congress finally outlawed them.

Fidelity pushed them in the military market and almost nowhere else.

When the sales practice was exposed, I offered Lynch a deal.

I offered to pay for Lynch to go to Iraq and take the place of a soldier who bought a Fidelity contractual fund.

I'm waiting for Lynch to respond.

Lynch might be inclined to grab my freebie if I were a Fidelity vendor. His lack of response may be because I'm not doing business with Fidelity and unlikely to be in the future.

There was a time when I sent Fidelity lots of business. When Peter Lynch managed the Fidelity Magellan fund.

Peter Lynch was the best mutual fund manager in the world. He had a reputation for integrity and honesty.

Something changed. Lynch retired as Magellan's manager and became Fidelity's Vice Chairman. He started hanging out with Hollywood pals like Lily Tomlin. He was in a position to know that Fidelity was peddling contractual funds to the military. He did nothing to stop it.

Squeezing profits out of soldiers never made sense. Fidelity is a huge company and the military is a small market. Fidelity sold the funds long after the unsavory practice was uncovered by the media.

In light of the Securities and Exchange Commission's case against Lynch, I now understand.

Lynch and Fidelity were blinded by a culture of greed.

Lynch set a poor example. As Walter Ricciardi, deputy director of enforcement for the Securities and Exchange Commission, said after Lynch's settlement, "the tone is set at the top."

Vice Chairman is as close to the top as you can get.

Fidelity's traders received more than $1.5 million in gifts, travel and entertainment. A 2005 *Wall Street Journal* article described a party in Miami that included Fidelity traders.

Party goers were supplied with private jets, female escorts and illegal drugs (ecstasy). The vendors paid for a party activity called dwarf tossing.

After you've done some ecstasy and thrown a dwarf across the room, you can probably rationalize peddling high priced funds to soldiers.

As far as I know, Lynch was not at the bash in Miami, but the Fidelity culture was set when Lynch started bumming free tickets.

When a top dog starts hustling freebies, it easy for others to justify it, too.

It becomes also easy to forget that soldiers buying contractual
mutual funds are being sent off to war.

Even though the SEC fined Fidelity $8 million, I still don't think that
Lynch gets it.

Doug Bailey, a spokesman for Lynch, told the *Wall Street Journal*
that the 14 Ryder Cup tickets Lynch improperly received, "had some
real historical significance to Mr. Lynch because he used to caddy"
at the course where the event was held.

I used to work on the cleanup crew at the Kentucky Horse Park. I
wonder if Lynch can get me 14 tickets to the 2010 World Equestrian
Games? That would have some historic significance for me.

To help my sense of history, I would like a private jet available to
me. I can skip the drugs, "escorts" and dwarf tossing.

If Lynch can rationalize his Ryder Cup freebies, I can justify jetting
with the rich and famous. I used to clean up after them.

And their horses.

Peter Lynch is grubbing for a handout. He sent a signal that
everyone at Fidelity could looks for handouts, too. Or push improper
products to soldiers.

As Mr. Ricciardi said, "It sets a tone."

I wish the SEC would have put me in charge of Lynch's punishment.
He would have gotten his one way ticket to Iraq.

That would definitely set a tone. A tone that would snap Fidelity's
managers in line. They would stop taking advantage of soldiers.

And tossing dwarfs.

Section Eight

The Scissor Sisters and Babydaddy's Daddy
(2004)

"All the young dudes
Carry the news"
-Mott the Hoople

The number one musical group in England is an American band called Scissor Sisters. They have a platinum album, open concerts for Elton John and sell out their individual shows. Soon, they will return to their home country and will be met with the same excitement and enthusiasm that greeted The Beatles.

Their musical leader and producer is Scott "Babydaddy" Hoffman of Lexington. Scott's parents, Phil and Nancy Hoffman, are dear friends of mine.

I became personally connected to Scott when I was invited to his Bar Mitzvah. Although Scott's thank-you note is worth a lot of money on eBay now, the Bar Mitzvah was an important point in my life for another reason.

It was the first Bar Mitzvah I was ever invited to. I had managed to make it through my first 30 years without much exposure to religions and cultures different from my own. By inviting me to share in a precious ritual of their faith, the Hoffmans broke down a barrier in my life. The Bar Mitzvah marked a turning point: it was then that I began making friends from diverse backgrounds.

In a recent *Lexington Herald-Leader* interview, Scott described his parents as conservative. A young rock star might think that, but in my opinion, they are liberal and open-minded.

Phil is a medical doctor. In fact, he is my doctor, and the model for what every doctor should be. He is calm and caring, and he knows his stuff. I've never waited more than 30 seconds in his lobby for an appointment, and his staff is first-rate. The medical profession would do well to study Phil and operate like he does.

Nancy has served in many political campaigns as well as on boards of civic groups committed to social justice. I've attended so many events with Nancy over the years that some refer to her as the "other woman" in my life. She is devoted to all three of her sons and is very active in their upbringing.

I've left out one tidbit about Scissors Sisters: three of the men in the group, including Scott, are openly gay. Moreover, their music draws on the influence of other gay or bisexual performers such as Elton John, David Bowie, Queen and the B-52's. Their sexuality is an important part of their act. In fact, one of their best songs, "Take Your Mama Out," is a about a gay man coming out.

I'm sure that Scissor Sisters shocks some people, but rock-and-roll has always been about pushing the envelope of social acceptability. Elvis Presley shocked audiences of my parents' era, just as David Bowie and Alice Cooper did when I grew up.

Phil and Nancy are the perfect parents for a son who is breaking down social barriers. They have spent their lives fighting prejudice and social injustice, and now their son is making a social statement with his music.

Each year at his first football practice, Coach Bear Bryant used to have his players call home and thank their parents for raising them. Bryant believed that people don't get to high stations in life without help. As Hillary Clinton said in a famous book, "It takes a village."

Scissor Sisters' unique sound was achieved through the talents of Scott and the other group members, but—at least in Scott's case—that genius was encouraged by two loving parents. Nancy and Phil could not be more supportive. In fact, Nancy's picture is in the video for "Take Your Mama Out," and Phil regularly monitors the band's message board.

"Babydaddy" is very lucky to have the mother and father that he has. They are part of the reason that he is headed for tremendous success.

Oral Roberts and Me
(2005)

"Now there are some preachers on TV
With a suit and a tie and a vest
They want you to send your money to the Lord
But they give you their address"
-Hank Williams Jr.

As an eighth grader in a Catholic school, I was given a challenging assignment. If I wrote a business letter that got a response, I got an A on the project.

My Baptist grandma was a huge fan of televangelist Oral Roberts. I was watching with her when Roberts said he always responded to anyone who wrote to him.

I wrote him, got my A and was on his mailing list for nearly 20 years.

Thus started 30 years of people writing to ask me for money.

I found that magazines sell your name to affinity groups. In high school, I subscribed to *Rolling Stone* which sold my name to every left wing group in the world.

I was still getting letters from Brother Oral and many pictures of his prayer tower. I even got return envelopes (Brother Oral never forget to send a donation envelope) with pictures of the prayer tower on the inside flap.

Along with that, I got daily mail from left wing groups.

I would get letters from groups saving whales, groups saving baby seals and groups wanting to save me, the whales and the seals away from nuclear reactors.

The letters had the same message as Oral Roberts: "send us money."

During my senior year in high school, Oral Roberts University made a big effort to recruit me. After five years on the mailing list, they must have felt that I was part of the Oral Roberts family.

I had to be the only long haired Democrat from a Catholic high school in Kentucky they had ever pursued. I still might be.

It was tempting as no other school wanted me. I was a lousy student with little money and schools would reject my application within seconds.

Then I started telling people I was an Eskimo.

It happened by accident. I was taking some kind of national test and there was a voluntary question concerning race. Since it was supposed to be voluntary, I left it blank. That did not suit the proctor, who insisted I check the Caucasian box. I refused and checked the box for Inuit Americans instead.

My mother swears she did not have a secret Eskimo lover, but I was angry about being forced to answer a "voluntary" question so the Inuit designation stayed.

I was flooded with mail from colleges wanting to recruit one of the few Inuit Americans living in Kentucky. Oral Roberts University suddenly had competition.

I wound up at Eastern Kentucky University which did not care about my grades or lack of Inuit heritage.

Although Oral Roberts eventually stopped writing, liberal groups persist in mailing to me.

I got a letter from Senator John Kerry last week. It listed a variety of world problems and then asked for $1000. He did not say if or how he was going to solve the problems, but sending him $1000 would somehow make things better.

Brother Oral was smoother. He wrote me nice letters, sent autographed pictures and never sent less than 10 pictures of the prayer tower. I never sent him any money, although I was tempted when he said he was going to die without it. But I rooted for the school's basketball team and felt like we had a connection.

I suspect that few of Oral Roberts' followers voted for John Kerry. Part of the reason might be ideology, but I suspect that those who have received mail from Brother Oral are used to high quality letters. They had to be thinking if Kerry sends out garbage when he is asking for $1000, what kind of stuff will he send out as President?

I'm not worried about John Kerry being President. He blew a golden opportunity and Democrats want him to go away. Even if he sends nice letters, people are going to ignore him.

Oral Roberts suggested that prayer might be the answer to some of the world's problems. Kerry just listed a bunch of problems with no solutions.

Oral Roberts should have run for President instead. At least he had a plan.

Celebrity Jeopardy

(2004)

"I lost on Jeopardy, baby"
-Weird Al Yankovich

I have had people question whether or not writing this column would take time away from my business and cost me money.

The column is part of a master plan to bring me great riches.

I need my column to make me a celebrity and then for Alex Trebek to allow me to participate in *Celebrity Jeopardy*.

When that happens, great riches are mine. If I can't clean up on *Celebrity Jeopardy*, every high school, college and graduate school that I have attended will revoke my degrees in shame.

Whether or not my grade school would allow me to hang on to my certificate is debatable.

For the uninitiated, *Jeopardy* is one of the world's most popular quiz shows. It brings fairly intelligent people on the show and asks them fairly intelligent questions.

Then two weeks out of a year, they bring on fairly unintelligent celebrities, ask them questions that a third grader could answer and watch the celebrities failure to answer them.

The greatest disillusionment is to see an actor who plays an intelligent character exposed as a complete idiot when they hit *Celebrity Jeopardy*.

The best example is when the cast of *Law and Order* showed up. The guy who is the lead prosecutor plays a serious and pious attorney with good sense and judgment.

On *Celebrity Jeopardy*, the man did not remind you of an educated lawyer; he reminded you of a guy who quit showing up for class somewhere in junior high. His character on the show has no sense of humor, and he does not look like a fun-loving guy. However, on *Celebrity Jeopardy*, the man decided he was a comedian. A really bad comedian. The kind they used to bring a big hook out for in vaudeville.

I'm dying to get on the same show as him. I know I can clean up if he is the competition.

Of course, a lot of how you do on *Jeopardy* depends on the categories you get. If I get on and the categories are Kentucky basketball, annuities and 1970s popular music, it will be a big night for me. A slight shift in categories to North Dakota basketball, grain futures and cello music would put me out of the game.

Even getting the category right can be tough depending on the questions. One night the final question on regular *Jeopardy* was about vice presidents. I have a master's in political science from Vanderbilt, and my thesis advisor, Michael Nelson, is the world's leading authority on vice presidents. I've read numerous books on the subject and used to be able to name every one.

I did not know the answer, which turned out to be Tipper Gore. Not only have I met Tipper on several occasions, I was one of Al Gore's state coordinators when he ran for president in 1988. I've met his entire family.

Maybe I should not be so hard on the *Law and Order* guy.

In my defense, the questions on *Celebrity Jeopardy* are a little less taxing than the one I missed playing along with real *Jeopardy*. Instead of being asked to give the maiden name of the vice president's wife, celebrity contestants field deep questions like "What is the name of George W. Bush's father?" and "What sport did O.J. Simpson play?"

Of course, you have to consider that the celebrities are rich and that they are playing for a charity. The charity is guaranteed a certain amount, no matter how badly the celebrity screws up. Thus, the "celebrity" episodes lend themselves to moments like when the *Law and Order* guy showed up and tried his hand at being a stand-up comedian.

My strategy for riches is based on the idea that Alex Trebek reads the *Richmond Register*. I don't know if he does, but there is always a chance. When he turns to my column, he will recognize that I need to be on *Celebrity Jeopardy*.

When I win, I will lord over the *Law and Order* gang, dance, do the Icky Shuffle and pull out a cell phone to announce the win to my friends. The act will make me as famous as Paris Hilton. As long as I am matched up against them, I can take home the money in buckets.

It all comes down to Alex reading the paper and calling me. I have not gotten in touch with the circulation department, but I will have to consider an alternative plan for fame and wealth if it turns out Alex is not a reader.

Celebrity Jeopardy may be the quickest way to cash in, but there have to be some other alternatives as well.

I'll be looking for them while I wait for the call from Alex.

The Yoko Ono Factor
(2003)

"Oh Yoko, oh Yoko
My love will turn you on"
-John Lennon

Prejudice and bias exist in the business world. There are some deep-seated prejudice and bias that cannot be explained with rational argument, thought or action.

I call this the Yoko Ono factor.

The Beatles came to America when I was four years old and were the musical soundtrack to my childhood. All of my friends were caught up in Beatlemania at its worst. The Beatles were my life.

When I turned 10, they were gone. I blamed this on Yoko.

People who study the history of The Beatles note that a lot of factors played into their breakup. There were creative differences, jealousies and the fact that George Harrison had developed as a songwriter along with Lennon and McCartney.

None of this mattered to me. I dumped all of the blame on Yoko.

Admittedly, Yoko was a good target. She was strange, even for the 1960s counterculture era. John helped her launch her singing career, which sounds like the noise a cat would make if its tail were caught in a lawnmower.

She and John did things like stay in bed for a week with the idea that this would bring world peace. Although I see the Internet these days offers plenty of people doing a lot of things in bed, none, not even Kim Kardashian, attach any goal of widespread social change to their actions.

Yoko did and it made me hate her even more.

I spent most of my teenage years hoping that John would see the light, dump Yoko and The Beatles would go right back to dominating the music scene. That did not happen and on December 10, 1980, Mark David Chapman took that chance away forever when he murdered John Lennon.

Lennon's death hit me like the death of a loved one. My friends and I sat and played "Imagine" over and over again for days. Although I was grieving, I could not extend sympathy to Yoko, John's true love. The prejudice had gone that far.

It has been over 30 years since John was taken from us. George has died, too. There is no way The Beatles could get back together, and I still can't warm up to Yoko. I suspect I never will. Short of Yoko coming to my house and hanging out under an expressed promise not to break into her singing voice, there is not a scenario where I can find Yoko endearing. It is just too hard.

I've spent all of my life fighting against discrimination based on race, gender, sexual orientation, size and appearance (I'm fat and don't like for other fat people to be discriminated against), and yet I understand how bigotry develops because of my issues with Yoko Ono. I see how it can take generations for change to happen and logic and rational thought to win out.

In the business world, the Yoko Ono factor has significant consequences when people cannot make smart choices because of irrational factors. I was watching a biography of Colonel Sanders and found that since he did not believe owning stock, his secretary, who did believe in it, made more money on Kentucky Fried Chicken than he did. People in business see it every day. People who don't believe in stock or real estate even when those have been proven to be great long-term investments. People who "don't like insurance companies" even when insurance would provide needed protection and annuities have shown to be great investments with tax advantages.

There are Yoko Ono factors that pop up in everyone's life in every circumstance. My dad refused to play cards with anyone who smoked a pipe. He could not explain why.

I guess knowing why is the key. If you understand why you have a bias and where it comes from, it is easier to get rid of your personal Yoko Ono factor in your life.

If I got to know Yoko, I suspect I would probably like her. She was a part of one of the greatest music stories of the 20th century and is a close link to an important part of musical history and history in general. The Beatles had a dramatic impact on popular culture and Yoko was there for all of it. We would probably wind up being friends.

As long as she promised never to sing.

The Saga of My Engagement
(2011)

"I've been around the block a time or two
Done almost everything a boy can do
I've done some living, yeah I've had fun
But there is one thing that I haven't done
I want to know how forever feels"
-Kenny Chesney

My friend, Dave Lieber, proposed to his wife via a column in the *Fort Worth Star-Telegram*. It became the title his popular book, *The Woman of My Dreams but the Dog of My Nightmares*.

I decided that I didn't want to plagiarize Dave. I developed my own proposal plan.

I took my then-girlfriend, Karen Thomas, to Jeff Ruby's restaurant in Louisville.

Jeff was a dear friend of my father and a pallbearer in Dad's funeral. He is now one of the most successful restaurant owners in the region. I knew that Jeff would provide the perfect dining experience for a proposal.

Karen agreed to marry me, but we had a couple of bumps along the way.

On the online reservation form, I had checked "Anniversary" because I wanted a private booth. I didn't want to make my pitch in front of someone leering from the next table.

Got the private booth. But the hostess, the waiter and the staff at the entrance kindly greeted us with their cheerful wishes of "Happy Anniversary!"

When Karen asked what anniversary they were talking about, I told her, "The first one." Then, I tried to give her my pitch, which I had written out in my semi-legible handwriting.

After three or four attempts to read it, she finally grabbed her reading glasses, figured out what I was fumbling around about, and, blessedly, said, "Yes."

I felt like I'd won the lottery. And I was handling it a lot better than Powerball Jack Whitaker or some of the other "Lottery Losers" I sometimes write about.

She later got up to use the ladies room. On her way back to the table, she slipped and fell and broke her thumb.

We made it through dinner, but spent the rest of the evening tracking down an urgent care center, getting X-rays and a cast. She had surgery shortly after.

I knew she really had to be hurting because normally she shakes off pain better than Sylvester Stallone in the early *Rocky* movies.

Karen grew up on a dairy farm. Cows have to milked and fed, 365 days a year. Nobody got a day off, even if they were sick. She is now the principal of a large Catholic school in Lexington where she doesn't want to hear about aches and pains.

She will have her ring to remember our special moment. And she will also have her thumb. I'm sure it will seem funny someday, maybe after the cast comes off.

We found a ring she liked and I purchased it. I stunned her by getting down on one knee, presenting the ring and again asking her to marry me.

It wasn't the question that stunned her. It was that with my age and body type, I was able to get down on one knee. She was even more surprised that I was able to get back up. Proving that, like Toby Keith, I may not be as good as I once was, but I'm as good once as I ever was.

Karen and I come from very different backgrounds. Her father is a successful dairy farmer in Cecilia, Ky., (close to Elizabethtown) and her mother is a retired school teacher. Her parents and siblings have college degrees and beyond.

My father was a professional gambler in Northern Kentucky. Until this May, I was the only McNay to graduate from college and the first to graduate from high school.

Karen is media-shy. She would never brag on herself. I operate in a totally public spectrum. I tell the world about my finances, my weight, my family and what I think about the chairman of the Federal Reserve Board.

It would never occur to her to write a public statement about our engagement. It would never occur to me not to.

We are both very independent and have been single for several years.

During that time, she raised three wonderful children. An accountant by training, she made a career move into education. For a couple of years, she made the 200-mile round trip from Winchester to Cincinnati, two or three days a week, to get her Montessori certification and Master's in Education from Xavier University. She then taught at a private school. Along the way, she got her Rank One and Principal's Certification from the University of Kentucky.

She writes for well-known education publications, speaks at national education conferences, and for many years served as Principal at Christ the King Elementary School in Lexington.

She didn't need me "to complete her." Her life was complete without me.

I stay happy and busy. But, as Kenny Chesney noted, the idea of knowing "how forever feels" has an overwhelming appeal.

I look at my most successful friends and at my oldest daughter and son-in-law. They are in stable and happy relationships.

Most of my friends have been married for a long time—or, at least got the right partner on the second try. Their marriages are partnerships built on love, sharing and trust.

When you start thinking about merging families, households, incomes and what to do with the pets, (her dog hates my guts; her cat worships me as an ally against the dog), it can seem simpler to stay single.

Then I look at how she adores me—which is truly a reflection of how I adore her.

So it all goes back to the Tina Turner question, "What's love got to do it with?"

In this case, everything.

I am finding out how forever feels. So far, it feels really, really good.

Unbridled Etiquette
(2005)

"Don't you know about the new fashion honey?
All you need are looks and a whole lotta money"
-Billy Joel

Mark Hebert at WHAS TV in Louisville did a story about the Kentucky Labor Cabinet hiring a consultant to teach their employees proper manners.

The employees were told they needed to bathe daily and wear real gold and silver instead of the fake stuff.

The consultant said that "conservative dress was a symbol of conservative political beliefs."

The story made me angry. I'm still mad about the state firing park workers with long hair and tattoos. I thought this was another example of Fletcher's team treating state employees like servants at their country clubs.

Then I realized the problem. The consultant did not understand the techniques necessary to work in state government.

Instead of telling employees to take a bath, she needed to be teaching things they really need to know.

For example, there is a proper way to greet a government contractor. A state employee needs to use phrases like "money is no object" and "your wish is my command" in the presence of any contractor who contributed to the Governor's campaign.

Otherwise, the employees will find themselves fired or transferred to Paducah. Proper manners can save a state employee's career.

The Governor's political staff needs to follow a different code when dealing with contractors. They should extend the right hand for a firm handshake and keep the left jacket pocket exposed so the contractor can stuff a wad of checks in it.

A political staffer should always wear a suit or jacket. Preferably one with big pockets.

Many people have seen guests who will not leave a party at the proper ending time. The manners consultant may have addressed that situation in her training.

State supervisors need to know how to ask people to leave state government jobs so that the Governor's friends can take their places.

The term for a person staying late at a party is called a "straggler." The term for someone trying to keep a merit job is called a "Democrat."

There is a proper way to deal with both.

With a "straggler," you should walk the guest to the door and hope they politely leave.

With a "Democrat," you should transfer them to a job far from their homes and hope they politely retire.

I'm not sure if the manners consultant discussed written communications. A handwritten note is an important social tool but email is gauche.

There is a penalty called the "indictment" for those in state government who make this social faux pas.

An indictment is almost as serious as not being listed on the social register.

Holding a door open is a part of good manners. Governor Fletcher showed his mastery of etiquette by putting in a secret door to his office. The $5000 door was seen as a waste of taxpayers' money, but actually was the first step in helping the Governor follow proper social procedures.

Instead of encountering an ill mannered reporter, who may or may not have bathed, the Governor can avoid contact with that ilk.

It would probably be a good idea to add a secret door to the Franklin County courthouse so that the Governor's staff can avoid reporters as indictments are handed down.

Bad manners breed bad manners, and the Governor's staff does not want to fall to the level of reporters.

Especially since few have a reporter wearing a Rolex.

If any of the Governor's appointees are convicted of a crime, it will send all their manners training right out the window.

The consultant for the Labor Cabinet said that conservative dress is equated with conservative thought.

Bright orange prison jump suits send the wrong fashion message. People will think they are radical, liberal Democrats.

Being seen as a Democrat would be harder on the Fletcher people than a stay in the big house.

They won't be able to flash real gold and silver in jail, and I am not sure if daily bathing is part of the routine.

If Fletcher staff people are convicted, they will have to add a special new etiquette program.

Maintaining good manners as they make "Unbridled Spirit" license plates.

IM HOLDING OUT FOR A HERO

Thank You Single Moms
(2012)

"I am a living legacy to the leader of the band"
-Dan Fogelberg

Mother's Day has normally been melancholy for me. My mother and sister died in 2006, the same year my marriage ended. After they died, my nephew moved to Kentucky to live with me while he attended college at Eastern Kentucky University.

My mother and his mother were single mothers. We weren't the Brady Bunch or the Waltons; our moms were all we had.

On 2007, Mother's Day hit on my sister's birthday, which also happened to be the anniversary of my crumbled marriage.

My nephew is an uber-macho guy, but suddenly started crying. When he started, I joined him for the rest of the day.

No tears this year. I used the day to reflect on what a terrific role model my single mother was.

And why Mother's Day is a 365 days a year position for single mothers.

I'm surrounded by a lot of terrific single mothers. I am marrying one in a few weeks.

In the past 10 years, she raised three children, became a highly acclaimed school principal and obtained a series of advance degrees and education honors.

I figured that after all that, she can tolerate my egocentric traits, or at least some of them.

My youngest daughter has raised my 11-year-old grandson as a solo act. A key staff member is doing her first Mother's Day as a single mom.

None of them complain about how hard it is; they just do it. The way my mother, Ollie McNay, did.

I was too young to appreciate the sacrifices my mother made. She went from being a homemaker in a comfortable suburb to loading boxes at night in a potato chip factory.

During the day, she went to nursing school.

Once she became an operating room nurse, she had the steady income and steady career to raise us. It also meant that she worked insane hours and normally missed major holidays.

Mom wasn't a "soccer mom." I didn't play soccer and if I had, she didn't have time to attend. She was lucky to catch a football game now and then.

Her focus was to keep us in our house, in a nice neighborhood, and to pay for me to attend a terrific Catholic high school.

The tuition was about 10 percent of her net income. I suspect she did it by juggling credit cards and all the things I tell you not to do in my *Wealth Without Wall Street* book, but it put me in a position to receive a high powered education and successful career.

Thank you mom. I wish I had been mature enough to thank you then.

It's easy to bash on the next generation as being self-absorbed, unable to communicate and happier interacting with technology than people.

Then I see the children of the single mothers who touch me.

My fiancé's children spent the weekend fixing things around her house, doing yard work and gave her a big mother's day celebration. They truly adore her.

My daughter posted on Facebook that her 11-year-old son made her breakfast in bed. I never thought about doing something that sweet and meaningful.

My staff member and her near teenage son did a mother-son outing where he did a number of things to make his mom feel special. I would have never dreamed of spending a day or an out of town trip with my mom during my teen years.

Being the son of a single mother, I spent time feeling like I missed out.

I felt particularly isolated as one of the very few children of a divorced family in my neighborhood and schools.

I was lucky that my dad remained a strong part of my life, but divorce was a stigma that I felt every day.

Along the way, I embraced the idea that being "different" was the key to my success and happiness.

It's no accident that I fell in love with a single mother. They know how to give unconditional love in a way the average people can't.

Being a single mom was not really a choice. It was motivated by leaving an intolerable situation, losing most of her money and material possessions, and seeking a better life for herself and her children.

Just like my mother, it showed her that she had unique and special talents. It let her understand that she was smart, resourceful and has a work ethic that stuns and amazes people.

Like Nietzsche said, "That which does not kill us makes me stronger."

What I know is that single mothers are stronger than I am. They draw upon strengths they didn't know they had.

It's easy to say that I missed my mother on Mother's Day. Then I realize that she is part of me and always will be. Every day of every year.

Thank you mom.

Nursing Angels and an Update to *It's a Wonderful Life*
(2011)

"I need 10,000 angels watching over me tonight"
-Martina McBride

At Thanksgiving, I had a lot to be thankful for. I was engaged to the woman of my dreams and my third grandchild had just been born. I had written a best-selling book and assembled a dream team for allowing my businesses to grow.

Since then, it's been a lot of doctors and hospitals.

I had lost the ability to urinate.

During my first trip to the emergency room, they drained eight liters of water from my bladder and told me I was lucky to be alive.

They sent me home with a catheter attached. It has been my almost constant companion since then.

I saw an urologist and we thought it might be an infection. It wasn't. I spent a week or so with the catheter. When I tried to take the catheter out, I wound up back in the hospital.

The urologist convinced me to operate and take out part of my prostate.

He hit the jackpot of my deepest fears. Surgery is the top of the list.

I've had one other surgery—age five when I got my tonsils out.

My fear of surgery is magnified by 29 years as a structured settlement consultant, helping injury victims with their money.

I've seen a lot of things go wrong in hospitals. I had a client go in the hospital for a knee operation and come out with heart transplant.

Statistically, errors are rare, but I see the times when they are not. I have a heightened awareness of what can go wrong.

In an era of managed care and big chains, mistakes are made and people fall through the cracks.

I didn't want to be another one who fell through the cracks.

My second biggest fear is cancer, and especially prostate cancer.

My dad died of prostate cancer at age 59, and I watched him die a horribly painful death. I hit 53 in February. I fear that my genetic time bomb will go off when Dad's did.

Any time I hear of a prostate problem, my mind immediately goes to cancer.

The first day played into my fears. I got to a chaotic hospital early, and after sitting through several exams and several hours, I was sent home because of what appeared to be a scheduling mix-up.

They then scheduled me for Friday surgery and a weekend stay. That played into another fear. I've seen bad things happen because patients were overlooked by understaffed weekend crews.

I try to give myself an edge. I came to the hospital with an entourage that Elvis would have envied. I told my thousand of Facebook friends which hospital I would be at. Two doctors are good friends and they called and emailed for updates a couple of times a day. I stopped at church for a blessing and updated my living will.

I was ready for anything, but scared to death.

On the second try, the hospital staff fell over themselves, and I was the first person taken to surgery. I woke up a few hours later, attached to my now-familiar catheter. I had a rough night, which included a bad experience with one of the nurses.

Getting into it with a nurse was a traumatic experience.

I love nurses. My mother was an operating room nurse for 27 years, and my family and friends endowed a nursing scholarship at Eastern Kentucky University after her death.

It's impossible for me to not see my mother in every nurse I encounter. I treat them with the respect that Mom deserved and didn't always get.

After the horrible night, I tried to call and email someone to help me and possibly get me out of the place. Early in the morning. I couldn't find anyone.

Then the shift changed and my guardian angel arrived.

In the movie *It's a Wonderful Life*, George Bailey (Jimmy Stewart) had a guardian angel who was an older, prissy man named Clarence.

My guardian angel was an early-20s nurse assistant from Nicholasville, Ky., named Crystal Hamblin.

Once Crystal and the registered nurse she works with, Sydney Napier Thigpen, came on the scene, life got better.

Crystal is going to school to be a massage therapist, has a two-year-old and works in the hospital every other weekend.

Crystal is street-smart with tons of common sense. She is a source of calm, but she was dealing with a middle-age man who wanted to jump out of his skin.

She and I immediately became friends, and she walked me through some deep breathing exercises.

She helped me get out of bed and go to the bathroom, which the night nurse had refused to do.

She changed my gown that was full of blood, urine and vomit and changed my bed covers, which were full of the same.

The message hit me that little things are what life is all about.

Last month, I was worried about weighty world issues. At that moment, I just wanted to use the bathroom and to stop smelling my own vomit.

Sydney and I hit it off right away, too. Syd has the work ethic and concern for her patients that reminded me of mom.

Sydney was there on Sunday, when I went through the four most painful hours of my life.

I was excited on Sunday morning. The doctor told me I was leaving. My fiancé was there to take me home.

They took the catheter out, and all I had to do was urinate.

Which I couldn't do.

Crystal came back and tried to get me to relax. No luck. I started feeling the same pain that got me in the emergency room the first time. I told Sydney to put the catheter back in.

Which she couldn't do. I had a blood clot blocking my urine flow.

Syndney called in the head nurse, Jennifer Watson, and eventually they called in another. They worked for two hours as hard as humans can work. Sweat poured off them.

They tried numerous (very painful) methods, but could only get a partial clot removal. Finally, the resident surgeon showed up.

It looked like I would have to have emergency surgery.

I politely told the resident, William Rogers, that I had selected my urologist, Fred Hadley, because he came highly recommended from numerous sources.

I did not want to be operated on by a resident.

A lot of people would have been insulted; Dr. Rogers was not.

He calmly told me he had significant hands-on experience and would try six options with surgery being the final one. He told me each attempt would be painful and carefully explained each option as he did them.

The procedures were incredibly painful, and as the area was inflamed it got more painful each time. However, the fifth option worked. I could literally feel the clot breaking and my urine shot out like a fire hose all over my newfound friends.

Who didn't seem to mind.

I met with the urologist today.

I don't have cancer. At all. I ditched the catheter and hope I never see it again.

I've spent my life chasing fame and glory, trying to achieve great things. I've never been one to stop and smell the roses. This forced me to.

I've been stunned by the outpouring of love, prayers and support.

Just like George Bailey, I've lived a wonderful life and have not always appreciated it.

I reconnected with the power of prayer.

During the year that Dad was dying, I prayed every night. When I was going through pain on Sunday, I started praying again. It was comforting and gave me peace.

I found on Facebook that well over 100 people, of different faiths and backgrounds, prayed for me in their own ways.

It reminded me that prayer is a universal language.

I connected with some angels at the hospital. Crystal, Sydney and Jennifer will probably rarely get their names in the newspaper, but get to see every day how they make a difference.

I also connected with the angels of above.

Prayer had been missing from my life for years, and I was reminded of why it is a tenet of every faith in the world.

I am blessed in many ways. I am blessed with health insurance and disability insurance. Many people have no health insurance and even fewer have disability insurance. Time off work can wipe them out.

I go into the New Year with a new sense of purpose.

If I can use the fame and fortune I've accumulated and keep the spirit of my angels in the front of my head, great things can happen.

I needed a kick in the balls to remind me.

Or maybe, a more painful sensation just a few inches higher.

View from a High-Powered Lobbyist
(2013)

I graduated from college in 1981. At the time, my alma mater, Eastern Kentucky University, and Western Kentucky University were fierce rivals in football, basketball and everything else.

I came back into the world of journalism in 2004, and by then Western graduates dominated the media in Kentucky.

When one of the Western grads was gigging me about being one of the few Eastern grads in a top slot, I said, "Western has all the journalists, but the top lobbyists in the state are Eastern alums. Your grads get to write about it, but our grads get to call the shots."

That ended that conversation.

It was also a true statement. Year after year, the list of Kentucky's top lobbyists includes Bob Babbage, Hunter Bates, John Cooper and Gene McLean, who are all proud Eastern alums.

In recent years, Babbage has topped the charts every year.

Babbage is the one that convinced me that the art of lobbying can be a noble profession. Bob refers to his profession as being an advocate for a cause and using strategic planning to help that cause achieve its goals.

He nailed it for me when he said that being a lobbyist was a lot like his early career on Lexington City Council. You build coalitions to get things done.

Like any other field, lobbying can have good people and horrible people. If you read my third book, *Wealth Without Wall Street*, you would think that "Washington lobbyist" and "devil worshipper" were synonymous in meaning.

Maybe that was a little harsh.

I get concerned that lobbyists are paid by big corporations and not held accountable by the elected public. Then I realize that many journalists are paid by big corporations and not elected either.

A little reflection might be good before I cast the first stone.

Babbage is an advocate who can always get my time and attention.

Like any good insider, Bob has built a strong, long-term relationship with me. He has been one of my closest friends for 34 years and best man in my first wedding. He was also in the second one, over 20 years later. He was instrumental in helping me launch my structured settlement business, and I served as Treasurer, Campaign Chair and Press Secretary in his successful elections to Kentucky's Secretary of State and Kentucky's Auditor of Public Accounts.

He knows what I am thinking before I say it. And vice versa. I understood the unique traits that made Bob the top lobbyist.

Bob is fearless and possesses incredible energy. He is enthusiastic about everything he does and constantly looking to think outside the box. That energy and enthusiasm fires up everyone around him.

When we worked together, Bob constantly pushed me to broaden my thinking, expand my horizons and never be afraid of working with big dollars and important people. Traits that have carried over to this day.

Each of Bob's three children were born during each of his three runs for statewide office and his wife Laura made a transition from CEO of a health care company to the ministry. Providing for his family became Bob's overwhelming objective in life.

It's hard to argue with the results. I was with Bob when he was inducted into the Henry Clay High School Hall of Fame a few years ago, and he said, "It's hard to believe that a nerd like me produced three of the smartest and coolest kids you will ever find."

His oldest son Robert is doing international business in Southeast Asia after going to Vassar on a tennis scholarship, receiving an MBA from Virginia and doing a stint on Wall Street. Julie is at Vanderbilt, writing for the Vanderbilt Political Review and serving as an intern in the executive office of the Ambassador in London.

Like in England. Not the London in Kentucky.

Brian is going to Furman on a track scholarship. I'm not sure where all the Babbage children are going to wind up, but Bob is intensely motivated on giving them a big start.

He is also motivated to maintain a high level of integrity for his firm. It's a corporate-style environment focused on attracting corporate government relations people who talk their language.

I'm not sure why so many of Eastern grads wound up as successful lobbyists. Babbage, Bates and Cooper all served as student representatives on the school's Board of Regents and learned how to get things done at that level.

Whatever the reasoning, it's nice to know I have friends in high places.

And that I get to write about them.

Josh Hamilton, Battling His Demons
(2007)

"Devil's got me now
Gone and got me now"
-The Kendalls

I have a new baseball hero: Josh Hamilton. Hamilton has never played in the major leagues and did not play any baseball for four years.

He was an addict. He flunked drug tests so often that he quit bothering to take them. He started his road to recovery 17 months ago and the Cincinnati Reds are giving him a chance to make the team.

Josh Hamilton has battled something bigger than sports: he has battled his inner demons.

The Washington Post did a wonderful story about Hamilton. He was the very first player chosen in the 1999 baseball amateur draft by Tampa Bay. He was in a car wreck. While recovering, he became addicted to drugs and tattoo parlors at the same time.

He has kicked drugs. Getting rid of tattoos has been a lot harder.

Hamilton was out of baseball, blew through most of a multimillion dollar bonus and reduced to cleaning up at a small town baseball diamond. After all of that, he is only 25 years old and still has some of the amazing talent that made him the first player selected by a major league baseball team. He found Jesus, found treatment, goes to meetings and has a lot of people rooting for him.

I am one of them.

As a diehard Reds fan, it would be incredible to see him on the same field as Ken Griffey Jr. and Adam Dunn. As a diehard supporter of people with addictions, I want to see a Josh Hamilton as a role model for where the demons lose.

Hamilton's fight is a one day at a time. Addictions are always near, waiting to come back. Josh will need to keep battling for the rest of his life.

I don't know Josh, but pray that he makes it. Something tells me that he will.

Josh is not my only Cincinnati Reds hero. My childhood hero was Pete Rose.

Rose didn't drink or smoke. Gambling was his demon. I knew he gambled. Everyone in Cincinnati knew. If you read the Dodd report that the baseball commissioner published in 1989, the evidence was overwhelming.

Pete has never been able to face his demons. He whines, takes pot shots and makes excuses. If he had apologized in 1989, went to gamblers anonymous or treatments and went through the steps Josh Hamilton has gone through, he would have walked in to the Hall of Fame years ago.

Instead Pete lived a lie. He kept lying and denying that he bet on the Reds and got many of us to believe him.

I almost got into a fistfight with an elected official who argued Pete didn't belong in the Hall of Fame. I was willing to put up my dukes for Pete. No one else had made 4256 hits and probably never will.

Then he did something stupid and despicable. He finally admitted he bet on the Reds, but his motives were lousy. He did it to hype a book he had "written." He wasn't sorry; he was trying to make a quick buck.

Charlie Hustle was trying to hustle us. It didn't work. The book flopped and a greased path to Hall of Fame for Rose was put on hold, probably forever.

Most people now view Rose as a piece of garbage.

Even after the book fiasco, Pete has not taken steps to atone to all those people that he hurt. His outer demon is gambling, but his real demon is the inability to take responsibility for his actions.

The way Josh Hamilton has.

Josh did not have a "posse" of excuse makers the way Rose has. Pete's entourage apologized for his lack of an apology.

It may be keeping Pete from getting help. If the people around Rose really cared for him, they would have shown him some tough love 20 years ago.

Pete was the great hero of my childhood. He played the game the way it ought to be played.

He just screwed up in the game of life.

The downside of an addictive personality caught Rose a long time ago. He needs to fight those demons and make amends to those he hurt.

The way Josh Hamilton has.

I hope Josh is on the Reds roster on Opening Day. He can give Pete Rose, and the rest of us, a lesson on how to play the game of life.

History Teachers Who Don't Know History
(2004)

"Don't know much about history"
-Sam Cooke

About 20 years ago, I was asked to speak to a college business class. During my lecture, I told the class they should stop studying business and start studying history and English instead.

I was never invited back.

In business, one must understand where this market has been and where it is going. Through the exploration of history, a person can analyze these trends.

I have a passion for history, a fire that was lit by tremendous high school history teachers and college professors.

Chester Finn Jr., my former professor at Vanderbilt and an education guru, noted that only 31 percent of middle school history teachers and 41 percent of high school history teachers actually majored in history.

Several fields may be necessary for middle school teachers, but I am horrified at the poor percentage of high school history teachers with degrees in history.

Yet, I do not blame the teachers, but rather the administration who hired them.

During college, I continually met students who despised history. For me, hating history was like hating pizza or the American flag. It was hard to imagine someone who could not love history.

When I asked why, I learned that many had high school teachers with no background or interest in history. The "teachers" made their students memorize dates and random facts instead of teaching students history.

Students subjected to classes like these should be able to sue the school for malpractice and have the school administrators arrested for torture.

History is about great people, events and movements in life.

My two high school teachers, Tim Banker and Joe Hackett, could not have been more different. In comparison, Hackett and Banker were like salt and vinegar. On the surface they did not sound like a good combination; however, their taste for knowledge had me striving to become a better student and a fan of history.

Banker, an Irishman who was left-handed and funny, coached football and track. During my junior year, I became Banker's favorite student because I too was Irish, left-handed, funny, played football and ran track. Yet surprisingly, I was not a likely candidate for being the teacher's pet.

Entering my junior year of high school, I ranked 110 out of a class of 128. I played sports, but did not have natural athletic ability. My friends were comprised of the top five students in the class and the worst five students in the class. The police were on a first name basis with the bottom five and quickly learning my name, too.

Banker helped me become excited about history and school in general, and in the process, I became a good student and drifted away from the negative crowd.

On top of knowing his history, Banker was a great entertainer. Banker believed learning should be fun and his teaching methods never lead to a dull class.

However, there was nothing fun about my other mentor, Joe Hackett. I have never known a tougher disciplinarian than him.

Hackett had been a meat cutter in Covington, and did not graduate from college until he was nearly 50.

Hackett coached state champion baseball teams, and I suspect his talents as a baseball coach kept him from getting fired. Hackett, a registered socialist and teacher in a conservative Catholic school, challenged and intimidated all of his students, despite their social class and parents' connections.

Hackett stressed that the powerful must be challenged or they will trample over the rights of the less powerful. I never left his class being afraid to challenge authority. I was only afraid of him.

I was privileged to be the first person to receive an award named in his honor. Hackett and I stayed in touch for the rest of his life, but he was not my buddy; he was my teacher and mentor.

Every adolescent and young adult should have teachers like Banker and Hackett—teachers with passion who actually study and believe in what they are teaching. Instead of teachers who are scrambling to stay one chapter ahead of their students.

The song quoted above should be seen as entertainment rather than the theme song for the quality of history teachers.

If I were in charge of education, administrators who hired history teachers who didn't know history would only have to remember one date—their termination date. It would be listed under current events.

Autism and My Grandson's First Swim
(2012)

"O, I believe, fate smiled and destiny
Laughed as she came to my cradle
Know this child will be able"
-Natalie Merchant

My 11-year-old grandson took his first trip off the diving board tonight. Two weeks previously, he couldn't swim at all.

Seeing an 11-year-old swim is normally not a headline. But, my grandson has been diagnosed with Asperger's Syndrome, which is a form of autism.

Seeing him jump in the pool was better than winning the lottery.

Having a grandson who can't swim is a frightening experience. What happens if he falls in water? I have not swum in several years, but know I can. Could I get him to safety in case of emergency?

Now that issue is going off the table. He can make it to safety without me.

With a child with Asperger's Syndrome, it's the little things that mean a lot.

When he was first diagnosed, I spent a lot of time reading about Asperger's Syndrome and autism.

A lot of people with Asperger's wind up as Wall Street stock traders, professional gamblers or computer geniuses. There are some who believe that Bill Gates has a form of Asperger's.

I'm not expecting my grandson to grow up to be a billionaire like Bill Gates. I am hoping that he has a happy, normal and productive life—the same hopes every parent and grandparent has.

The first thing I learned about autism is that there is no such thing as a "cure." There is a lot of education and special training needed. You don't suddenly flip a switch or take a pill and have an autistic child fill in the gaps in how his mind is circuited.

People who have children with autism learn what they can, find all the support and programs available and give love to their child with everything they have.

Thus, it is easy to get excited when a grandson jumps off the diving board and takes a swim.

I was surprised recently to find that my grandson was suddenly "cured" of Asperger's Syndrome.

It didn't come from being struck by lightning or due to the efforts of a faith healer like Oral Roberts.

It came from the American Psychiatric Association.

When the next edition of the *Diagnostic and Statistical Manual of Mental Disorders* comes out, it won't list Asperger's as a diagnosis at all.

On the same day that my grandson made his successful leap off the diving board, the APA confirmed that it would maintain a new definition of autism, which will not list Asperger's as a possibility.

The irony is that for a long time he was unable to swim due to the sensory and motor issues associated with the disorder the APA is saying doesn't exist.

The "re-definition" by the APA came from a perception that Asperger's and other forms of autism were "over diagnosed."

In other words, according to the APA, the way to avoid paying for treatment is to suddenly decide that the disease doesn't exist at all.

That is an outrage that will keep thousands of children from getting help.

What happens when the children are 20, 30 and 50 years old and have never been counseled, educated or treated? A simple "change" in APA definition can damage children who could easily be helped.

My grandson is fortunate in one respect. Our family business, McNay Settlement Group, helps special needs children handle their money and plan for the rest of their lives.

His mother, aunt, and uncle are experts who know every financial vehicle and public program available to help children with special needs.

If health care reform is not overturned by the United States Supreme Court, several excellent new programs will be implemented to help autistic children.

There are a number of advocacy groups, such as Autism Speaks, that are springing up to help in this area.

My grandson and I recently went to a baseball game. He is learning about the sport his grandfather loves. While we were there, he completely reprogrammed my cell phone. He fixed a problem in 30 seconds that Apple's tech people couldn't fix in three hours.

He's a great child with a big heart. With a lot of love, education and counseling, "he will be able."

The jump in the pool was a big step forward.

One that caused his grandpa to leap for joy.

Al Smith and the Battle against Addiction
(2008)

"Say you'll be alright come tomorrow
But tomorrow might not be here for you"
-Lynyrd Skynyrd

The Society of Professional Journalists (SPJ) announced that legendary Kentucky journalist Al Smith will be named as a Fellow of the Society at their September convention in Atlanta.

Fellow of the Society is the highest honor SPJ bestows on a journalist for extraordinary contribution to the profession. Last year, Carl Bernstein (of *All the President's Men* fame) was named as a Fellow.

Al is running with the big dogs.

Although Smith, a former head of the Appalachian Regional Commission, is no stranger to the national scene, his greatest impact has been on the local and state level.

He understands the creed of helping people, one at a time and taking life one day at a time.

Al's story is incredible when you realize that he came from extreme depths.

He fought a severe battle with alcohol in the early part of his life. He lost numerous jobs in New Orleans and wound up in Russellville, Ky. There he stopped drinking, bought the paper he was writing for, bought some other papers and rose into greatness.

He made to the top by helping others. His demons were replaced by angels.

People battle different demons. Some more severe than others.

I've been fascinated by an Emmy winning television program called *Life or Meth* on A&E. I didn't know much about meth addicts before the series. I know more about them now.

I saw how meth hits close to home. They filmed part of the program outside my office. It doesn't get much closer than that.

It has been said that meth addicts are nearly impossible to cure.

My home county of Madison and neighboring county Clark are giving it their best shot.

They have a concept called Juvenile Drug Court or "drug court" for short. Judge Brandy Brown and Program Supervisor Anna Beth Hardiman are featured in the television program.

It looks like they are having some success.

Addiction is something that society has to come to grips with. Throwing addicts in jail is a dumb idea. It doesn't solve the problem or what drove them to addiction to begin with.

On the other hand, I can see the temptation to get people off the street, even temporarily, like Otis on *The Andy Griffith Show*.

Otis was never a threat to another's safety, but many addicts are. People who drive while impaired or commit violent crimes while high are a danger to everyone.

Some countries don't have addiction problems. They just shoot the addict.

We operate a little differently here.

If drug court can make a dent in the addiction problem, I want to know more about it and tell others.

I know what Al Smith would tell me: get out and do some digging.

See firsthand what is going on.

So that is what I am going to do.

I'm going to learn more about what drug court is about. I'll observe the process and interview the people involved. Then I'll write about the experience.

I normally don't do firsthand observation and journalism, but I want to get to the frontlines of the war against addiction and see what is going on.

For every person stumbling through an addiction problem, there is a potential Al Smith: Someone who can turn their lives around, turn other people's lives around and make an impact at the state, local and national level.

If we are going to progress as a society, we need to figure out how to find the next generation of Al Smith's, take them out of the grips of addiction and allow them to be productive.

We need to make some moves. Drug court is one of them. If we don't act, tomorrow might not be here for America.

Acknowledgments

*"She was a friend to me when I needed one
Wasn't for her, I don't know what I'd done"*
-Jackson Browne

My friends were both he's and she's, but I did not want to mess with a Jackson Browne lyric.

If you read any of my books, *Son of a Son of a Gambler: Joe McNay 80th Birthday Edition, Life Lessons from the Golf Course, Life Lessons from the Lottery, Wealth Without Wall Street, Son of a Son of a Gambler: Winners, Losers and What to Do When You Win the Lottery* or *The Unbridled World of Ernie Fletcher*, you will see the names of the people who were there for me. That includes my wife, children, grandchildren and a plethora of terrific friends.

I have to give special mention to Adam Turner, Editorial Director at RRP International, who edited and designed this book. The eye-catching cover was his idea and this is the fifth bestseller that he has edited in his short but nonstop career in the publishing business.

McNay Scholarship

"Gimme some money, gimme some money"
-Spinal Tap

I've thought about a way to honor Dad. He was a generous man and believed in education.

Like many in my family, he was the product of a single parent household. People ask about my grandfather because of the book title, but really little is known about him. He died when dad was seven.

Dad would also be proud that my wife is President of a school like the Ursuline Academy, where the school has a strong tradition and history of giving back.

Thus, I've asked Karen to set up a McNay Family Scholarship at Ursuline. It will be given to a student, or potential student, who is from a single parent family and grasps the concept of "Serviam" or giving back to their communities.

In 2007, we were able to endow the Ollie and Theresa McNay nursing scholarship at Eastern Kentucky University. The vast majority of the money needed to endow the scholarship came in small donations from people who read the original book.

I'd like to be able to endow this scholarship in the same way.

To donate, please note on the check that the money is to go the:

McNay Scholarship at Ursuline Academy
Office of Development
Ursuline Academy
2635 State Street • New Orleans, LA 70118-6399

About the Author

Don McNay, CLU, ChFC, MSFS, CSSC
Best-Selling Author, Syndicated Columnist, Financial Consultant
www.donmcnay.com

Don McNay, an award-winning financial consultant and writer, is an expert in settlement planning and one of the world's leading authorities on how lottery winners handle their winnings.

His syndicated financial column appears regularly in *The Huffington Post* and in hundreds of publication worldwide. McNay also has appeared in several hundred television and radio programs, including *CBS Morning News, CBS Evening News with Katie Couric, ABC News Radio, BBC News, KPCC- Los Angeles, WLW-AM-Cincinnati, Al Jazeera-English, CBC Television* (Canada), *TBS eFM* (Korea), *RAI* (Italy), *CTV* (Canada) and *Radio Live* (New Zealand). His insight has been sought by hundreds of print publications, including the *New York Times, Los Angeles Times, New York Daily News, Tampa Bay Journal, National Enquirer, Reuters, Associated Press, USA Today* and *Forbes.*

McNay has written five best-selling books: *Life Lessons from the Lottery, Wealth Without Wall Street* and *Son of a Son of a Gambler: Winners, Losers and What to Do When You Win the Lottery* and *The Unbridled World of Ernie Fletcher.* His most recent, *Life Lessons from the Golf Course,* co-written with PGA Professional Clay Hamrick, was a bestseller as well. He is also the CEO and Chairman of RRP International, a book publishing company based in Richmond, Ky. and Greater New Orleans.

Entering the financial services business in 1982, McNay was a pioneer in the field of structured settlements, helping injury victims and lottery winners handle large sums of money.

He founded McNay Settlement Group Inc., which is part of the McNay Group (www.mcnay.com). The organization is considered one of the world's leading experts concerning structured settlements, mass torts and qualified settlement funds. His company has been noted for its work with special-needs children, along with injury victims and lottery winners.

A graduate of Eastern Kentucky University, McNay was inducted into the Eastern Kentucky University Hall of Distinguished Alumni in 1998. McNay has a master's degree from Vanderbilt University and a second masters in Financial Services from the American College in Bryn Mawr, Pennsylvania.

McNay is a Lifetime and Quarter Century Member of the Million Dollar Round Table signifying that McNay met the organization's highly selective standards for service, production and ethical behavior in 25 different years. McNay has four professional designations in the financial services field.

Don received the Certified Structured Settlement Consultant (CSSC) designation from a program affiliated with Notre Dame University.

He is a Chartered Life Underwriter (CLU), a Chartered Financial Consultant (ChFC) and earned the Masters of Financial Services (MSFS) designation.

Among his professional involvements are former Treasurer of the National Society of Newspaper Columnists and former Director of the National Structured Settlement Trade Association. He has spoken numerous times at structured settlement industry conventions. He sits on the Board of Directors for Society of Settlement Planners.

McNay has won several awards for his newspaper column, including "Best Columnist" from the Kentucky Press Association.

Don is a former Director of the Eastern Kentucky University National Alumni Association. He was named Outstanding Young Lexingtonian in 1985 by the Lexington Jaycees. He is an honorary Kentucky Colonel and named as an honorary Duke of Hazard by the Mayor of Hazard, Kentucky. McNay is a University Fellow at Eastern Kentucky University and a University Fellow at the University of Kentucky.

A prolific author and lecturer, McNay has spoken to hundreds of legal and financial groups throughout the United States, Canada and Bermuda. He has published research articles for *Trial*, *Round The Table* (the official publication of the Million Dollar Round Table,) *Claims Magazine*, *Best's Review*, *Trial Diplomacy Journal*, *National Underwriter* and other financial industry publications.

Don is married to Karen Thomas McNay, who is President of the Ursuline Academy in New Orleans, the oldest Catholic school and oldest all girls school in the United States. He has two children, three grandchildren and three stepchildren and raised his nephew after his sister and mother died in 2006. He lives in both Richmond Kentucky and New Orleans.

Comments about Don McNay during His Decade as an Award-Winning Columnist

"Don McNay is an original, provocative voice taking on all of those who would get rich off our ignorance and feelings of financial desperation."
-Gary Rivlin, *Newsweek/Daily Beast*, author of *BROKE, USA*

"Don McNay understands money...how to make it and, better yet, how to hang onto it."
-Ed McClanahan, author of *The Natural Man, Famous People I Have Known* and others

"At last, a road atlas to wealth for those of us who don't like driving on Wall Street."
-Byron Crawford, award-winning columnist, author, broadcaster and member of the Kentucky Journalism Hall of Fame

"Known for his simple, yet insightful, approach to money management, Don's road map to financial security is a must-read for all Americans searching for practical, long-term solutions to debt reduction and elimination, entrepreneurship and wealth-building minus the high-stakes gamesmanship of Wall Street."
-Renee Shaw, producer/host, Kentucky Educational Television

"I have known Don for 25 years and have enormous respect for his ability to find unique solutions to not only financial, but also other problems. We served on our association's board of directors (NSSTA), and Don was a voice for sanity when we were dealing with difficult issues (If only he were in Congress now).
-Len Blonder, Los Angeles, California; two-time past president of the National Structured Settlement Trade Association

"Don McNay combines deep understanding of his subjects with straightforward, clear writing and plain ol' common sense to help all of us think more clearly about the big issues."
-Judy Clabes, editor, KyForward.com; former editor, *The Kentucky Post*; member of the Kentucky Journalism Hall of Fame

"Don McNay has nailed it. In our changing economic climate, he has taken a complicated subject and made it easy to understand."
-Jim LaBarbara, member of the Radio/Television Broadcasters Hall of Fame, author of *The Music Professor, a Memoir*

"Don understands money, but his real strength is understanding people. He has real insight into what motivates the players and he explains it well to my audience. He's one of my favorite guests."
-Joe Elliott, Louisville, Kentucky, *The Joe Elliott Show*

"You don't have to study the labor disputes in professional sports, the misdeeds in college sports or the politics in Washington for very long to see there's a shortage of common sense. That's exactly what I found when I started reading Don McNay's columns several years ago. We brought him on our radio show at that time to talk about financial issues in a way that connected with people more than someone looking to come up with a great sound bite."
-Tom Leach, radio host and two-time winner of the Eclipse Award for broadcasting excellence

"McNay is a financial adviser and newspaper columnist.... He specializes in helping people who have come into sudden money."
-Joe Nocera, *New York Times*.

"Don McNay has consulted multiple lottery winners and offers primary pieces of advice."
-*Los Angeles Times*

"Reading Don's work is like having a conversation with an old friend; an old friend who's as proud of his rock n' roll record collection as he is of his investment portfolio."
-Samantha Swindler, publisher and editor, *Tillamook Headlight-Herald*, Tillamook, Oregon; winner of the 2010 Tom and Pat Gish Award for courage, integrity and tenacity in rural journalism

"Don McNay doesn't try to impress you with his knowledge; he cuts through all the Wall Street hyperbole and breaks it down into what matters most, dollars and 'sense.' His no-nonsense approach to money provides sensible, practical advice in a humorous fashion. He's one of my favorite guests, and I always learn something new."
-Neil Middleton, award-winning journalist, vice president of news WYMT-TV

"When Don McNay shares his remarkable experience and astute advice you can take it to the bank—literally. And you will be glad you did."
-O. Leonard (Len) Press, founder, Kentucky Educational Television

"I have been a big fan of Don McNay's for many years. Don's writing style is real pragmatic without the hyperbole. He writes for the everyday person in a style that's fun to read, with very sharp insights for everyday investors. Don has not been afraid to call out the big institutions, while sharing the benefits of terrific opportunities right in our own backyards."
-Keith Yarber, owner/founder, *Tops In Lex*

"Thank goodness there are still journalists like Don McNay left in Kentucky and America: fearless, truthful, compelling, and willing to take on powerful interests. He's what the First Amendment was all about two centuries back."
-John Eckberg, author of *Road Dog* and *The Success Effect*

"Don McNay came to journalism relatively late, but he quickly proved that he has some attributes of fine journalists--a nose for

news, a sense of justice, a capacity for outrage about injustice, a sympathy for the average person, a willingness to speak truth to power, and a sense of humor."
-Al Cross, Director of the Institute for Rural Journalism and Community Issues, based at the University of Kentucky, and political writer for *The Courier-Journal* for 15 1/2 years

"The claimed accomplishments of a political leader can only be measured with good and accurate information, and the consistent reports of Don McNay certainly provide that reliable news."
-Julian M. Carroll, Kentucky State Senator and Former Kentucky Governor

"Rock 'n' roll can parallel life and politics in ways that are funny, ironic, incisive and profound, and thus, Don McNay engages his readers. Lyrics from the likes of John Mellencamp and Melissa Etheridge spotlight McNay's tough topics, and McNay's research and plainspoken style enlightens."
-Suzette Martinez Standring, Syndicated Columnist, Past President, National Society of Newspaper Columnists and author of *The Art of Column Writing*

"In rapid time, Don McNay has emerged as a powerful voice for disempowered Kentuckians: men and women who work hard and play by the rules, but whose quest for a share of the American Dream is frustrated by corrupt politicians and special interests. May his voice continue to resonate."
-Jonathan Miller, Kentucky State Treasurer and author of *The Compassionate Community: Ten Values to Unite America*

"Thank God the SOB wasn't writing back when I ran for office."
- Rick Robinson, best-selling author, Fort Mitchell attorney, former congressional aide, and former congressional candidate

"Some people like to go to the track and catch a race or to the stadium and watch nine innings. They go with a pencil behind their ear—and they keep notes. They may curse the stumbling horse or the third baseman's sloppy glove. But they curse them out of love, as a

mother scolds a wayward child. Don McNay may love horses, he may love baseball. I honestly don't know. But I do know he loves politics, and he keeps notes. Like any true fan, his aspersions are from the heart. He only wants that horse to run like he did in the morning workout, that third baseman to catch like he did in the minors and that governor to govern the way he promised to in the campaign."
-Mark Neikirk, former Managing Editor of the *Cincinnati Post* and the *Kentucky Post*

"Don McNay is a keen observer of today's political, social and economic landscape. He writes colorfully, clearly, and with great humor. But more than that, he exhibits the courage to speak the truth no matter the consequences. Such courage is a rare commodity in today's world."
-Bill Garmer, Lexington Trial Attorney, Association of Trial Lawyers of America Governor and Former Chair of the Kentucky Democratic Party

"Don McNay is one of those fearless folks we all want to be. His writing is both wittingly disarming and courageously straightforward. McNay speaks and writes in a language we can all understand and never pulls punches. Taking on the establishment is easy; doing it with charm, style, and clarity of reasoned thought makes for a very good read."
-Alan Stein, former President, Lexington Legends Professional Baseball Team

Check out these other great titles!

27280437R00114

Made in the USA
Lexington, KY
03 November 2013